HAL•LEONARD
GUITAR
PLAY-ALONG®

modern BLUES

VOL. 166

ISBN 978-1-4234-4320-9

HAL•LEONARD®
CORPORATION

7777 W. BLUEMOUND RD. P.O. BOX 13819 MILWAUKEE, WI 53213

Guitar Notation Legend

THE MUSICAL STAFF shows pitches and rhythms and is divided by bar lines into measures. Pitches are named after the first seven letters of the alphabet.

TABLATURE graphically represents the guitar fingerboard. Each horizontal line represents a string, and each number represents a fret.

4th string, 2nd fret

1st & 2nd strings open, played together

open D chord

HALF-STEP BEND: Strike the note and bend up 1/2 step.

WHOLE-STEP BEND: Strike the note and bend up one step.

GRACE NOTE BEND: Strike the note and immediately bend up as indicated.

SLIGHT (MICROTONE) BEND: Strike the note and bend up 1/4 step.

BEND AND RELEASE: Strike the note and bend up as indicated, then release back to the original note. Only the first note is struck.

PRE-BEND: Bend the note as indicated, then strike it.

VIBRATO: The string is vibrated by rapidly bending and releasing the note with the fretting hand.

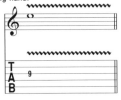

PALM MUTING: The note is partially muted by the pick hand lightly touching the string(s) just before the bridge.

HAMMER-ON: Strike the first (lower) note with one finger, then sound the higher note (on the same string) with another finger by fretting it without picking.

PULL-OFF: Place both fingers on the notes to be sounded. Strike the first note and without picking, pull the finger off to sound the second (lower) note.

LEGATO SLIDE: Strike the first note and then slide the same fret-hand finger up or down to the second note. The second note is not struck.

SHIFT SLIDE: Same as legato slide, except the second note is struck.

TRILL: Very rapidly alternate between the notes indicated by continuously hammering on and pulling off.

TAPPING: Hammer ("tap") the fret indicated with the pick-hand index or middle finger and pull off to the note fretted by the fret hand.

NATURAL HARMONIC: Strike the note while the fret-hand lightly touches the string directly over the fret indicated.

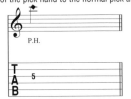

PINCH HARMONIC: The note is fretted normally and a harmonic is produced by adding the edge of the thumb or the tip of the index finger of the pick hand to the normal pick attack.

TREMOLO PICKING: The note is picked as rapidly and continuously as possible.

VIBRATO BAR DIVE AND RETURN: The pitch of the note or chord is dropped a specified number of steps (in rhythm), then returned to the original pitch.

VIBRATO BAR SCOOP: Depress the bar just before striking the note, then quickly release the bar.

VIBRATO BAR DIP: Strike the note and then immediately drop a specified number of steps, then release back to the original pitch.

Additional Musical Definitions

 *(accent)* • Accentuate note (play it louder).

 (staccato) • Play the note short.

D.S. al Coda • Go back to the sign (𝄋), then play until the measure marked "***To Coda***," then skip to the section labelled "**Coda**."

D.C. al Fine • Go back to the beginning of the song and play until the measure marked "***Fine***" (end).

Fill • Label used to identify a brief melodic figure which is to be inserted into the arrangement.

N.C. • Harmony is implied.

 • Repeat measures between signs.

 • When a repeated section has different endings, play the first ending only the first time and the second ending only the second time.

CONTENTS

Born with a Broken Heart

Words and Music by Danny Tate and Kenny Wayne Shepherd

Tune down 1/2 step:
(low to high) E♭-A♭-D♭-G♭-B♭-E♭

Intro
Moderate Blues ♩. = 111

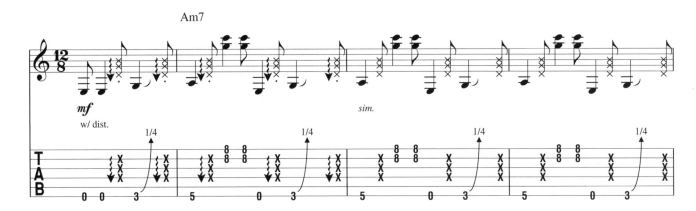

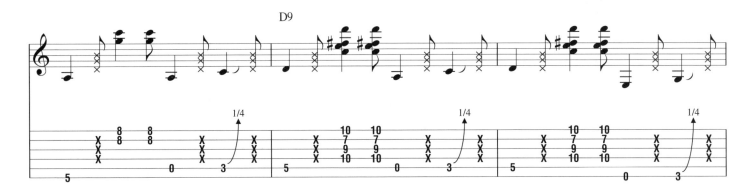

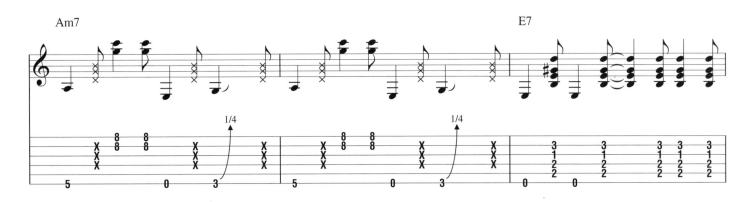

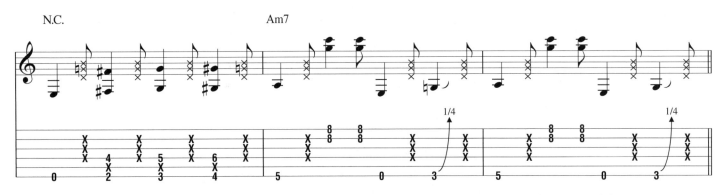

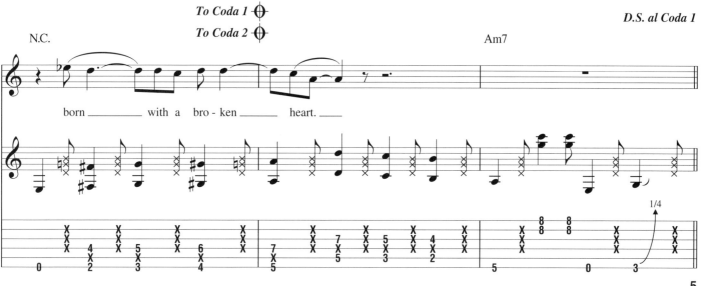

⊕ Coda 1

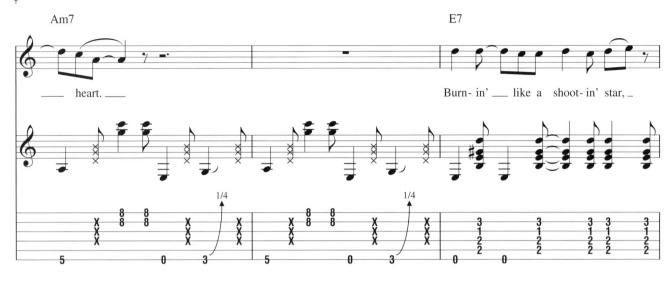

heart.

Burn- in' ___ like a shoot- in' star, ___

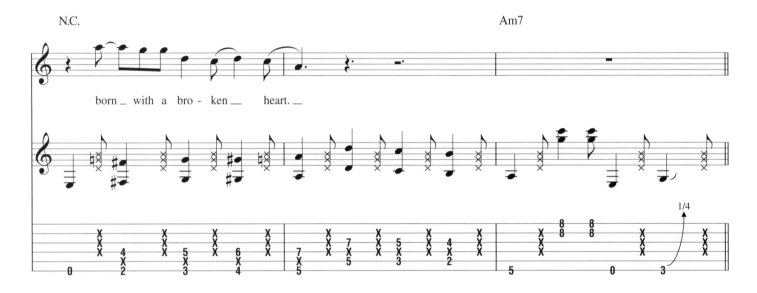

born ___ with a bro - ken ___ heart. ___

Guitar Solo

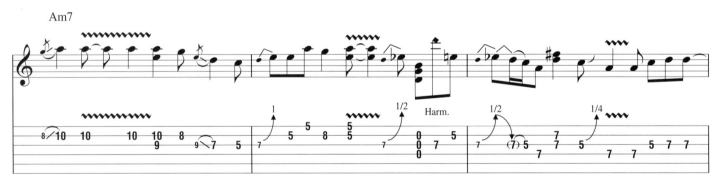

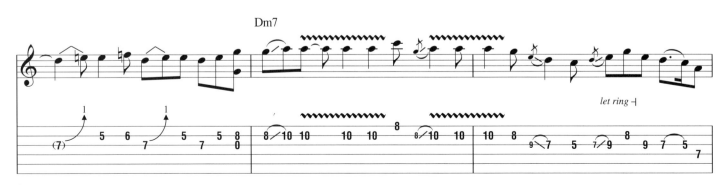

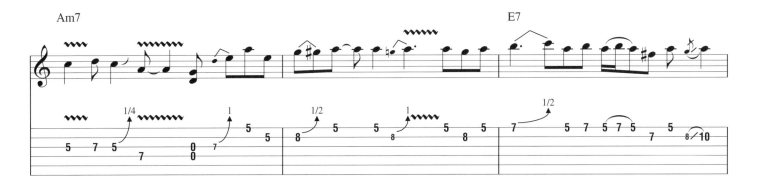

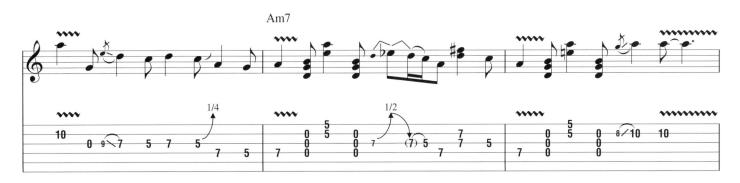

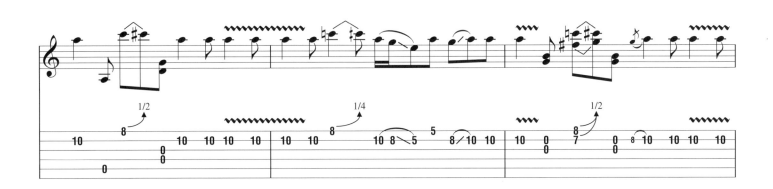

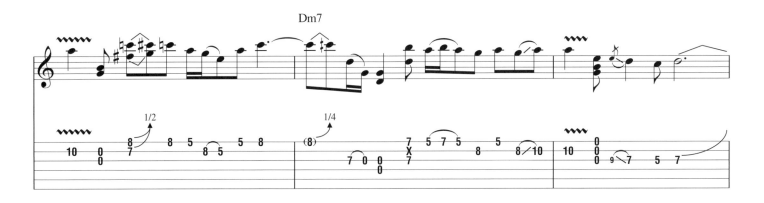

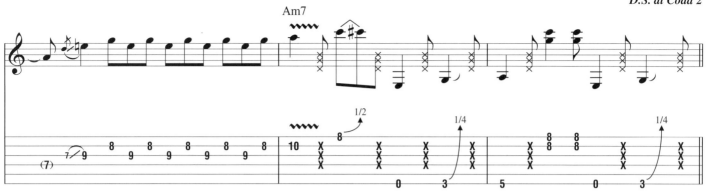

⊕ Coda 2

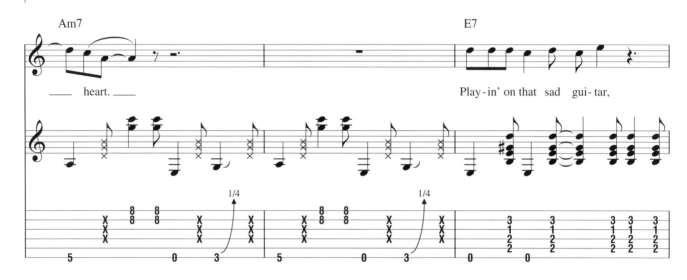

heart. ___   Play-in' on that sad gui-tar,

born ___ with a bro-ken ___ heart. ___

Burn-in' ___ like a shoot-in' star, ___   born ___ with a ___ bro-ken   heart. ___

Outro-Guitar Solo

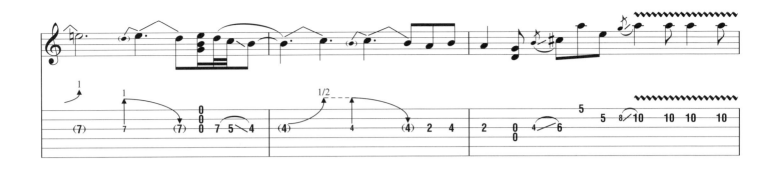

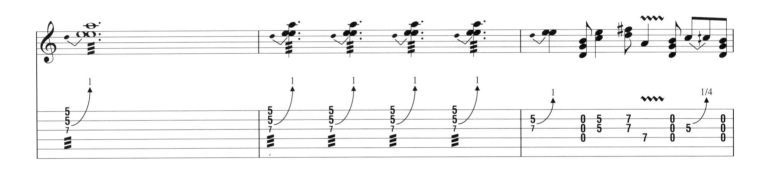

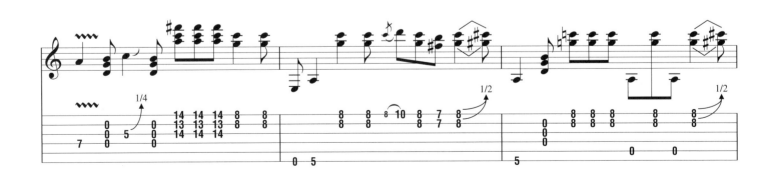

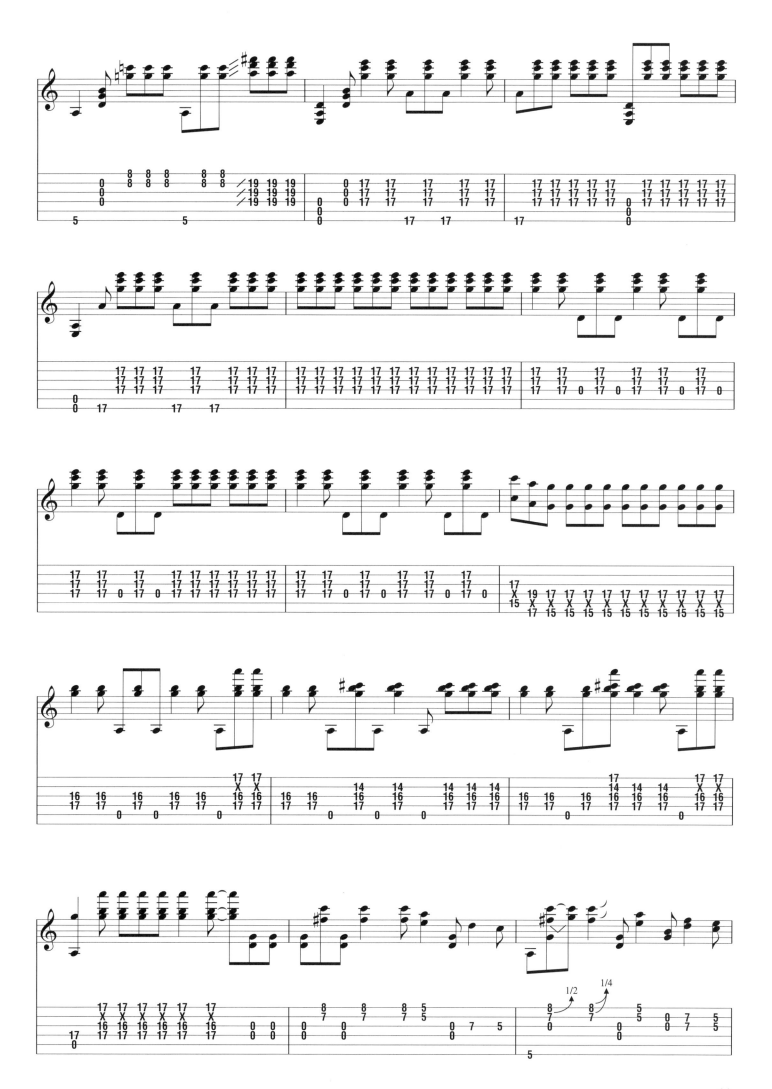

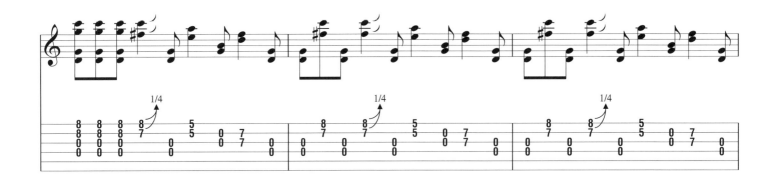

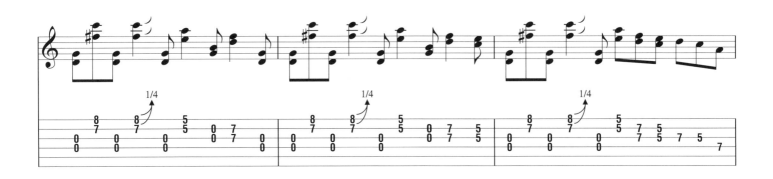

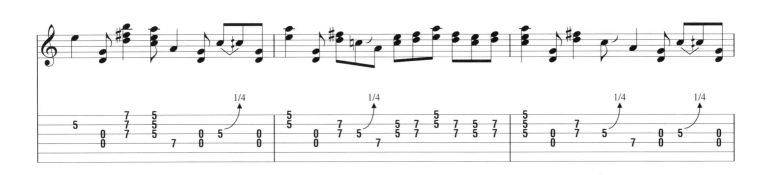

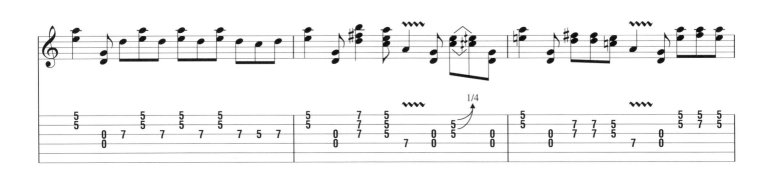

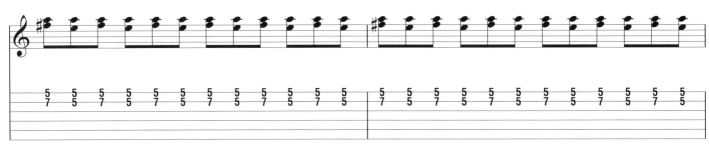

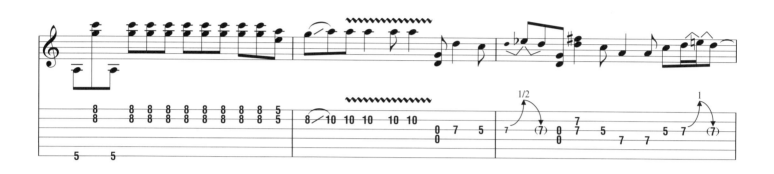

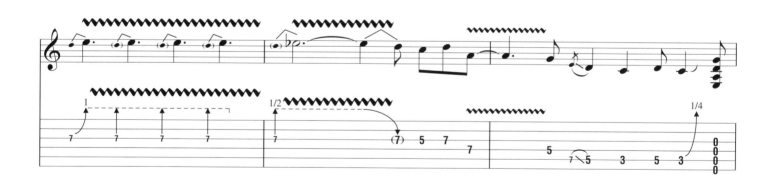

Additional Lyrics

2. Off in the distance, callin' my name,
   I took me a ride on a slow rollin' train.
   It still runs.
   It seems the good die young.
   Playin' on that sad guitar,
   Born with a broken heart.
   Burnin' like a shooting star,
   Born with my broken heart.

3. Seems it was over before it begun.
   Killed by a bullet from a six-string gun.
   Bang a drum.
   Oh, why do the good die young? Yeah.
   Ridin' in a long black car,
   Born with a broken heart.
   Playin' on that sad guitar,
   Born with a broken heart.
   Burnin' like a shootin' star,
   Born with a broken heart.
   Yeah!

Damn Right, I've Got the Blues

By Buddy Guy

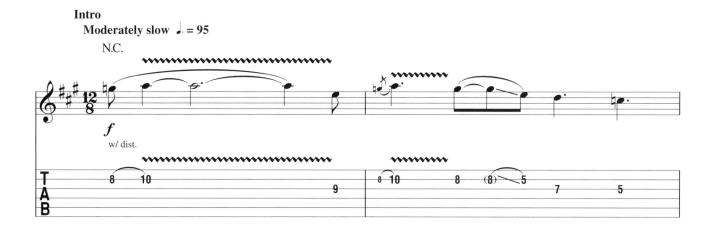

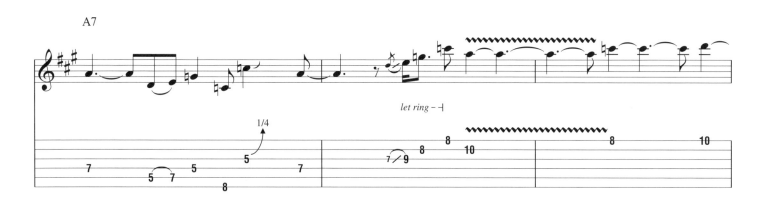

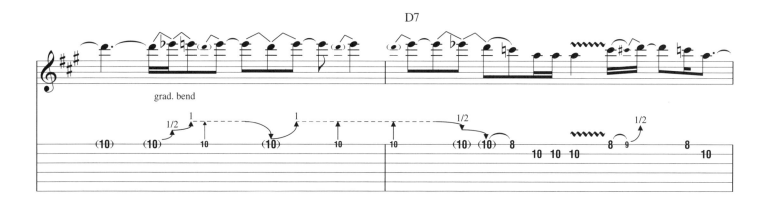

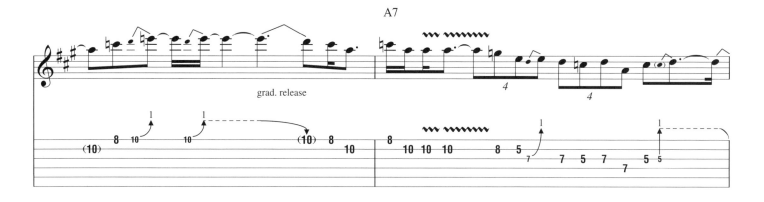

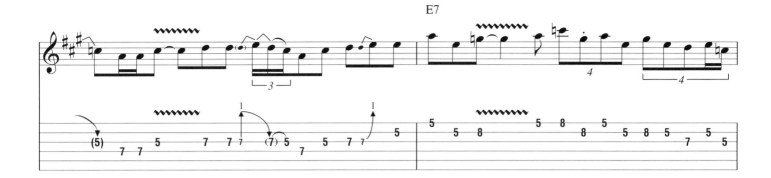

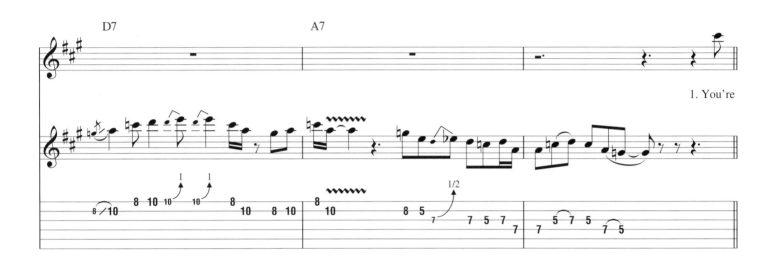

1. You're

𝄋 Verse

2nd time, substitute Fill 1

A7

damn right, I've got the blues _
3. You damn _ right, I've got the blues _____

from my head _ down _ to _ my shoes.

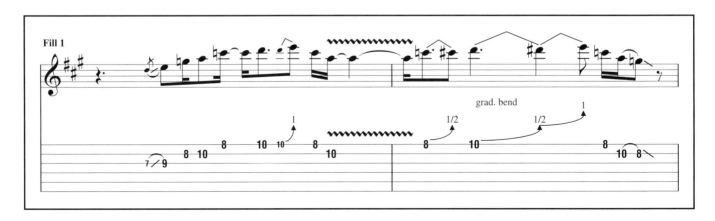

Fill 1

grad. bend

You damn right, I got the blues ___   from my   head ___ down ___ to ___ my

2nd time, substitute Fill 2

To Coda ⊕

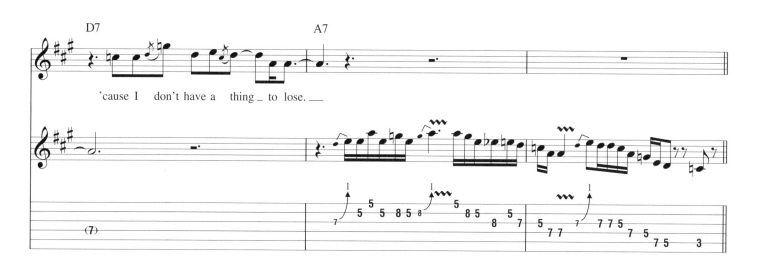

shoes.   I   can't ___ win _____

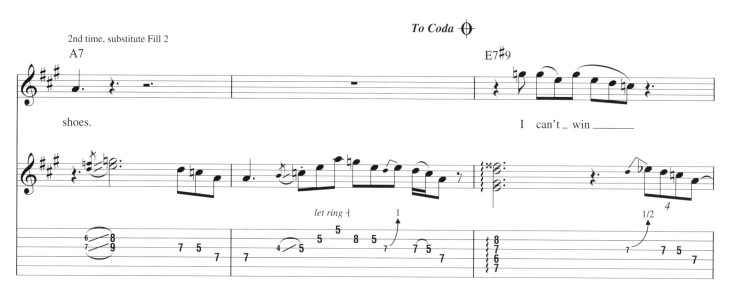

'cause I   don't have a   thing ___ to lose. ___

Fill 2

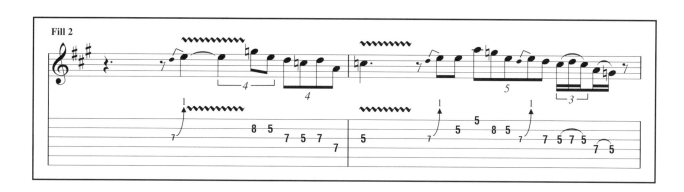

17

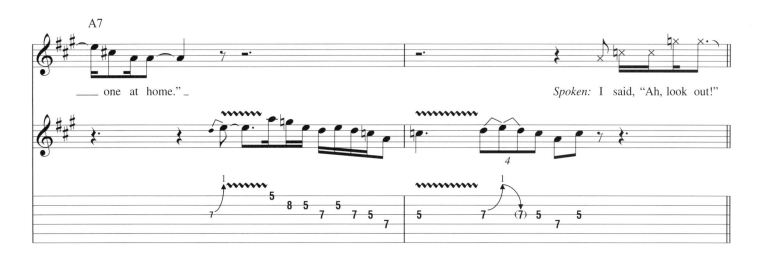

You know, my new grand-ba-by came to the door __ and say, "Grand-dad-dy, you know ain't no __

__ one at home." _ *Spoken:* I said, "Ah, look out!"

Guitar Solo

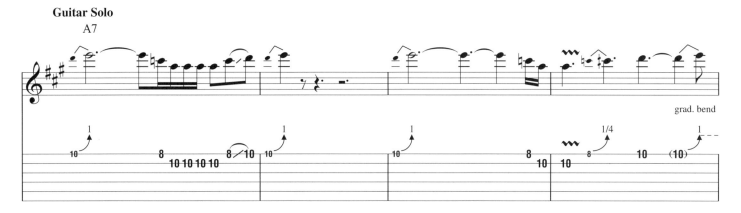

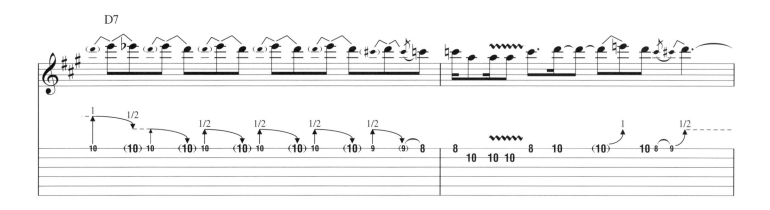

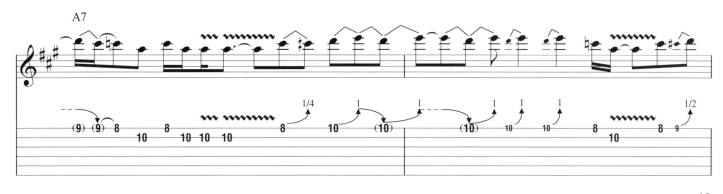

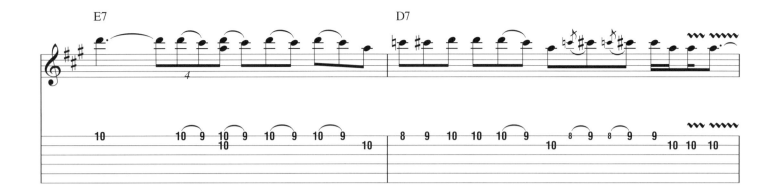

D.S. al Coda

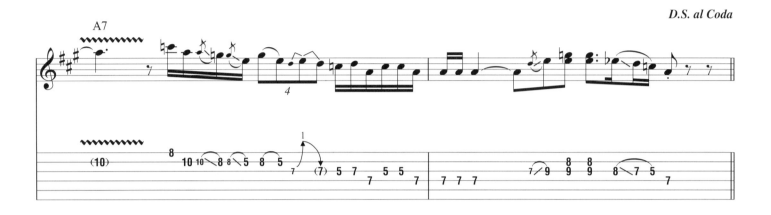

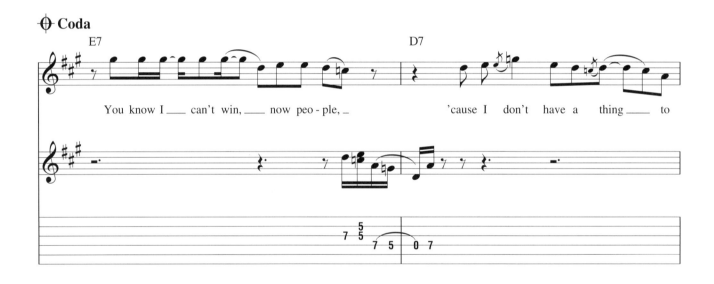

You know I ___ can't win, ___ now peo - ple, ___ 'cause I don't have a thing ___ to

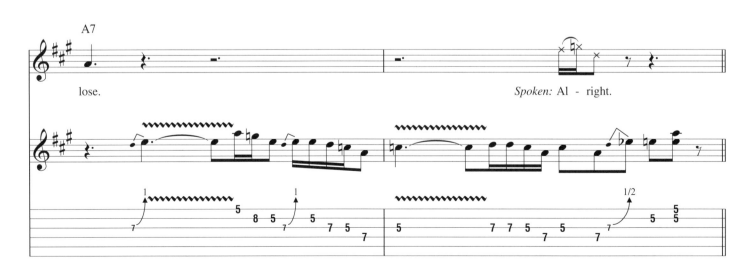

lose.

Spoken: Al - right.

Guitar Solo

A7

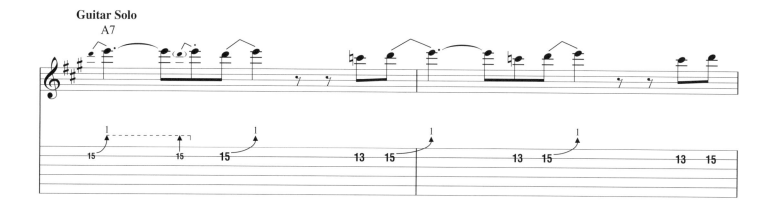

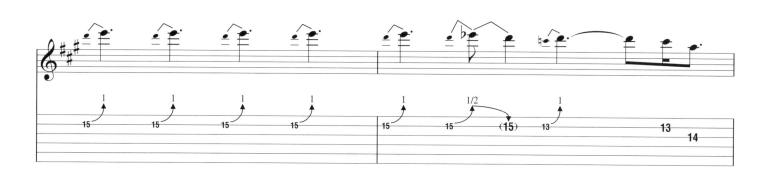

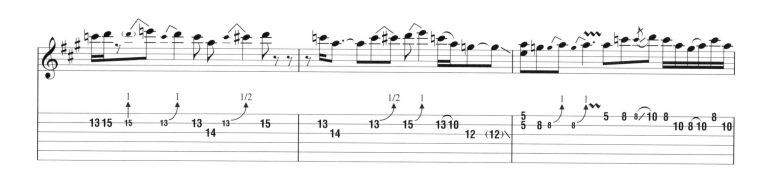

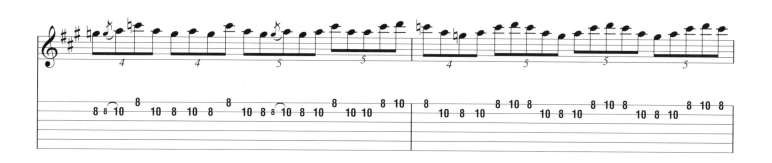

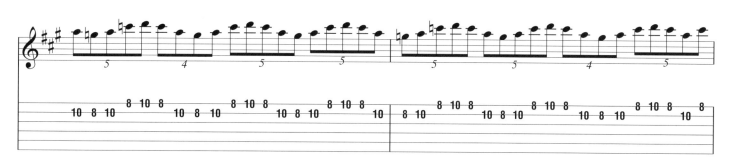

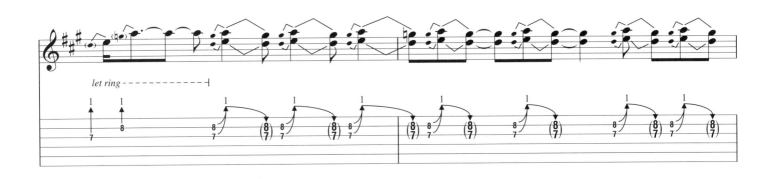

Outro

Gtr. tacet

A7

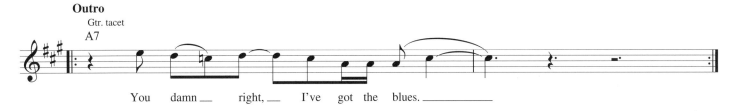

You damn ___ right, ___ I've got the blues. ___

You damn ___ right, ___ I've got the blues. ___

You damn ___ right, ___ I got the blues.   *Spoken:* Yeah. ___

Begin fade

w/ clean tone

Fade out

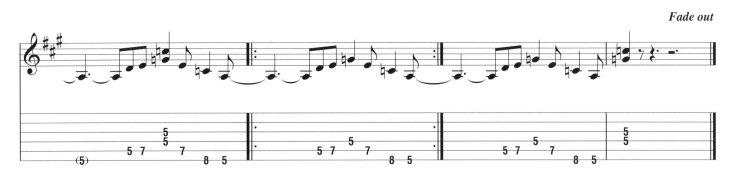

23

Lie to Me

Words and Music by David Rivkin and Bruce McCabe

Tune down 1/2 step:
(low to high) E♭-A♭-D♭-G♭-B♭-E♭

Intro
Moderately ♩ = 108

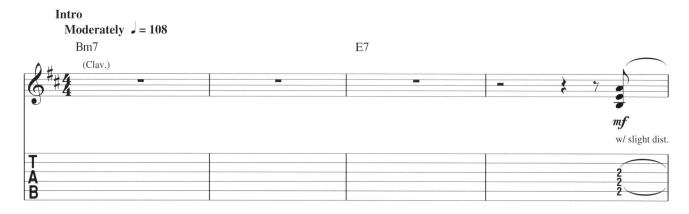

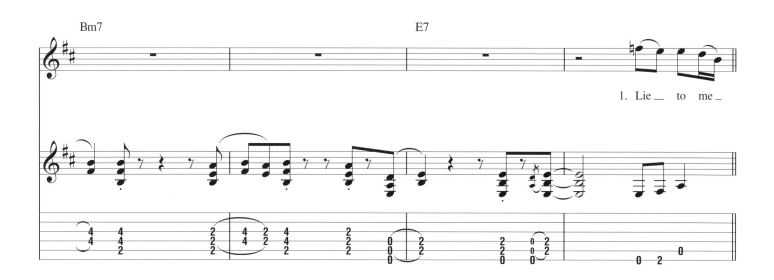

1. Lie __ to me __

Verse

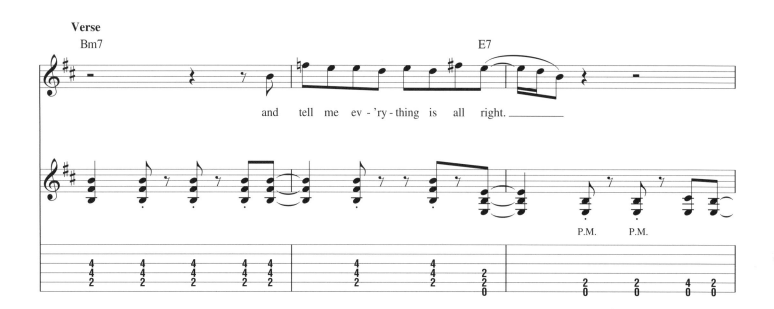

and tell me ev-'ry-thing is all right. __

P.M. P.M.

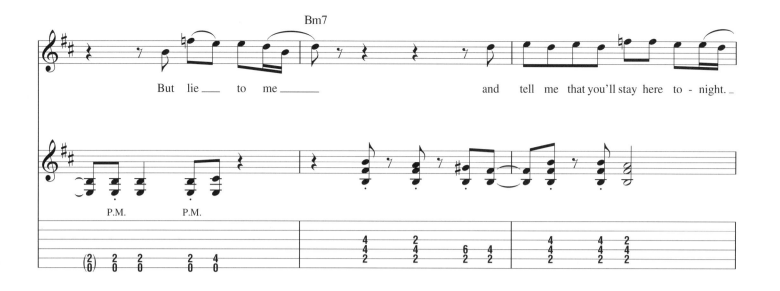

But lie ___ to me _____ and tell me that you'll stay here to - night. _

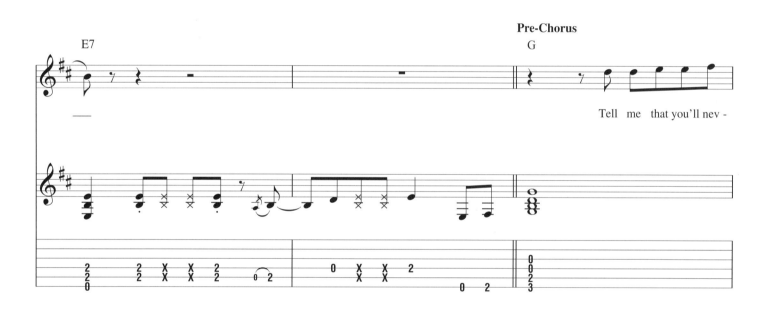

___ Tell me that you'll nev -

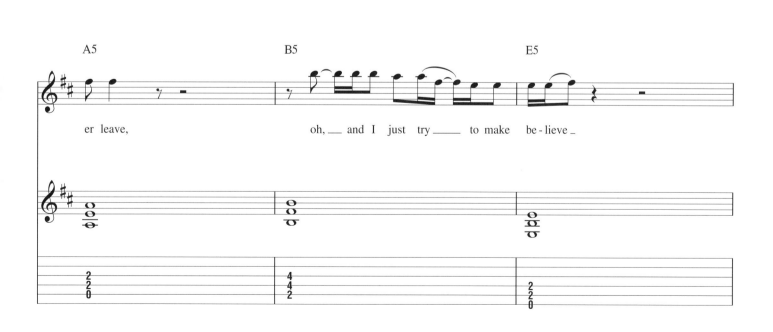

er leave, oh, ___ and I just try ___ to make be - lieve _

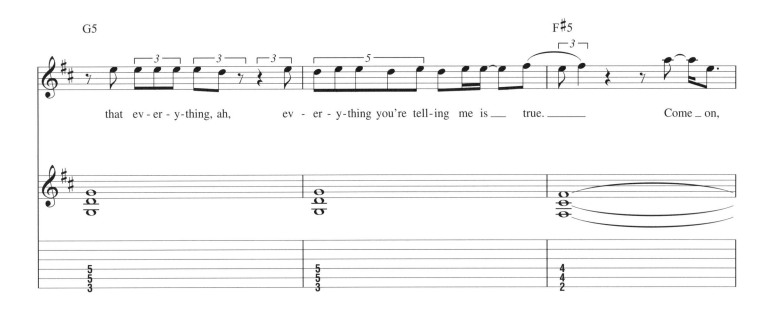

Chorus

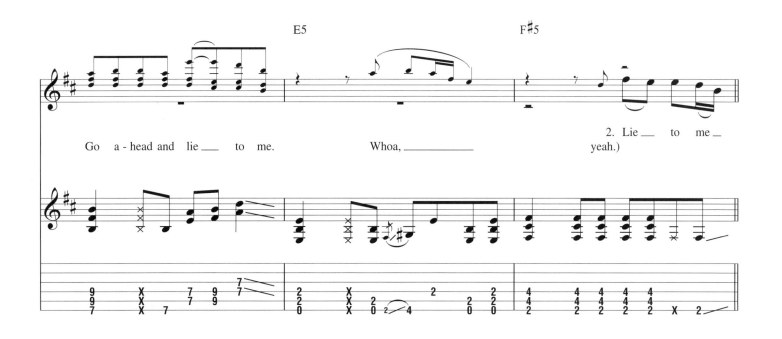

Go a-head and lie ___ to me. Whoa, _____ 2. Lie ___ to me ___ yeah.)

Verse

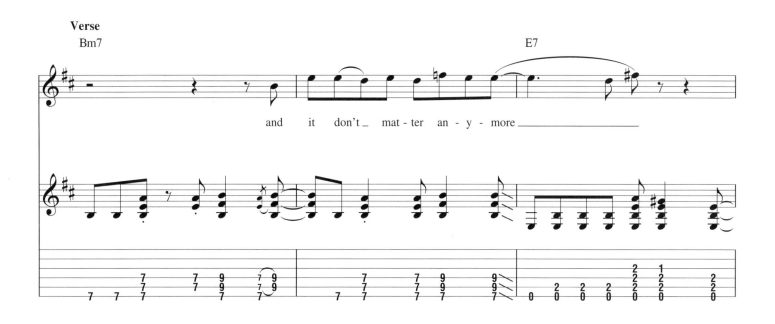

and it don't ___ mat - ter an - y - more _____

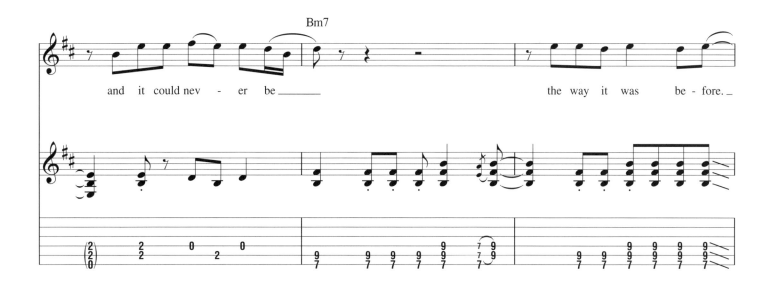

and it could nev - er be _____ the way it was be - fore. ___

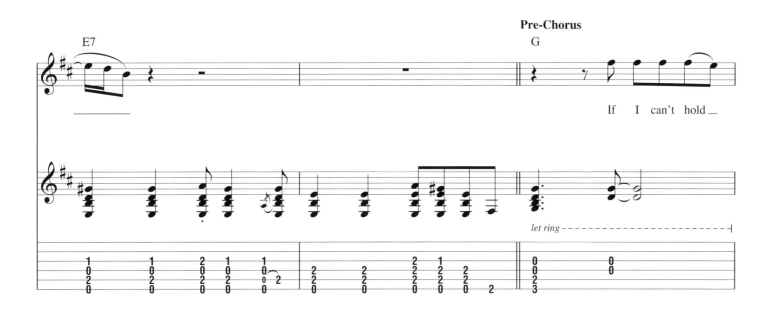

Guitar Solo

Come on   and...

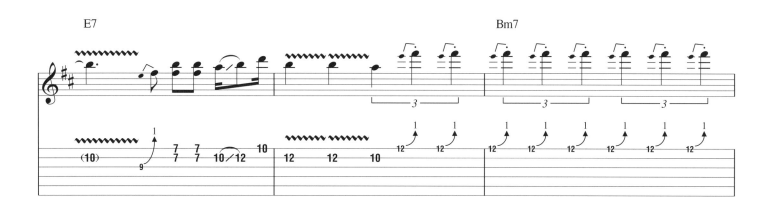

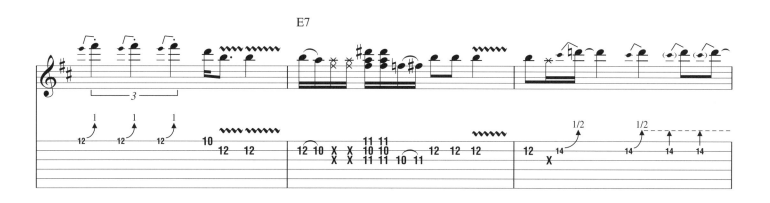

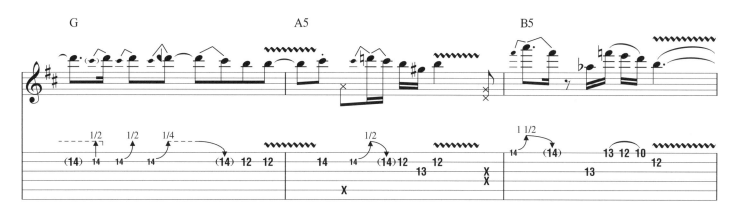

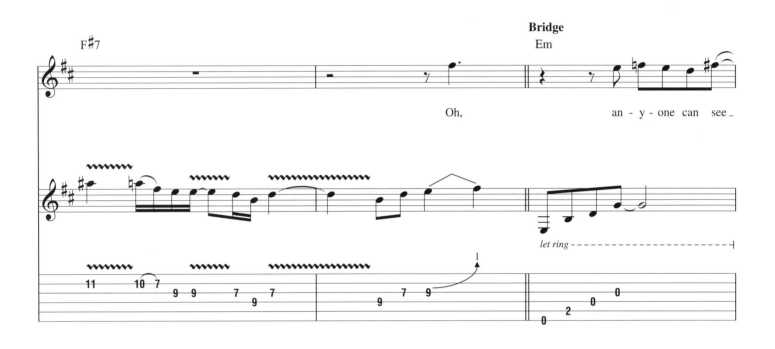

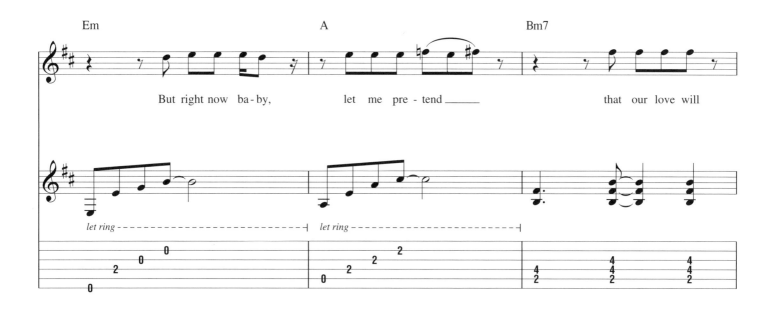

Em   A   Bm7

But right now ba - by,   let me pre - tend _____   that our love will

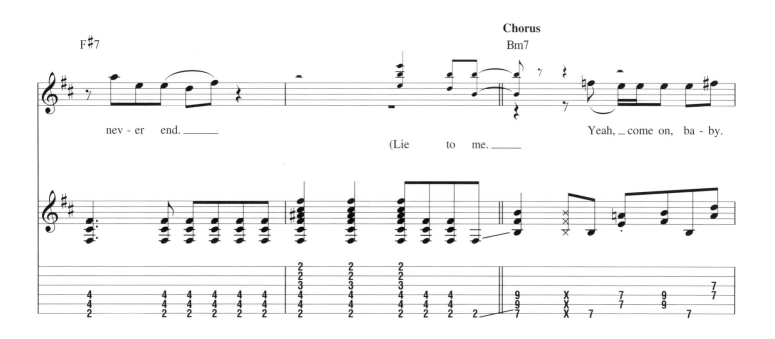

F#7   **Chorus**

                           Bm7

nev - er end. _____   Yeah, __ come on, ba - by.

(Lie   to   me. _____

                          E5   F#5

                      You know just what I'm talk - in' a - bout. ___

Go a - head and lie   to   me.   Oh, _____   lie   to me.

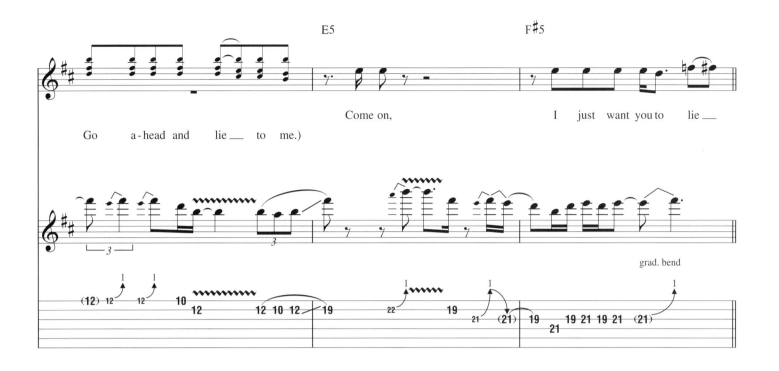

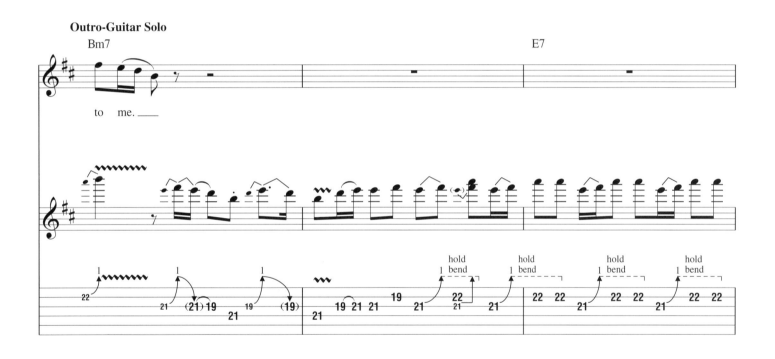

Outro-Guitar Solo

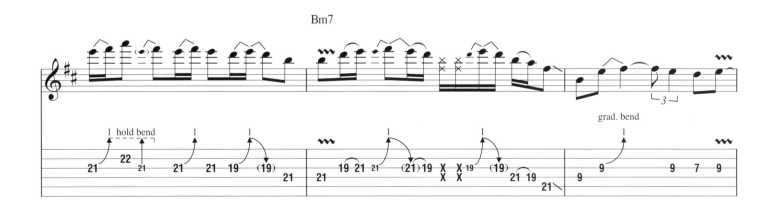

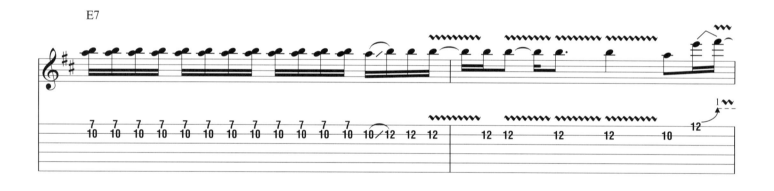

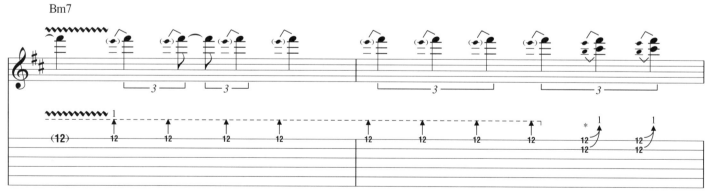

*Bend both strings with
same finger, next 2 meas.

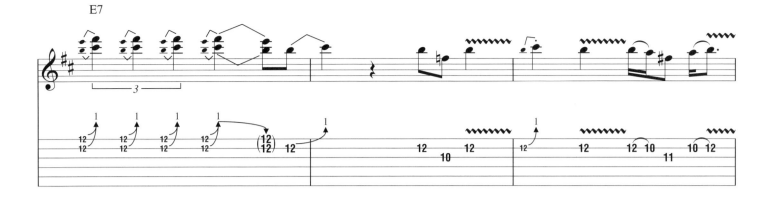

Begin fade

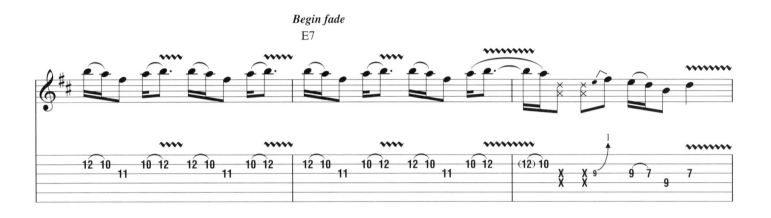

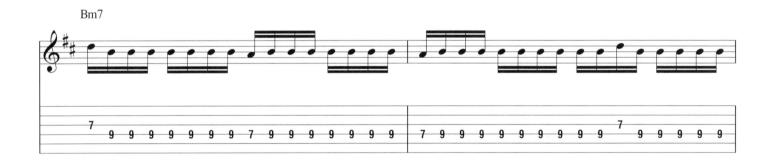

Fade out

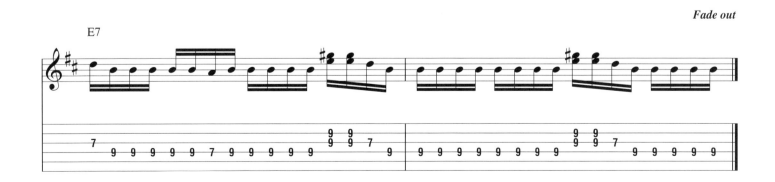

My Way Down

Words and Music by Chris Duarte and John Jordan

Tune down 1/2 step:
(low-to-high) E♭-A♭-D♭-G♭-B♭-E♭

Intro
Moderately ♩ = 98

Cm7

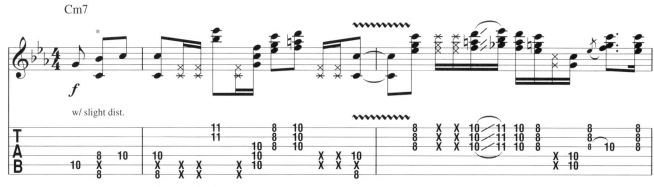

w/ slight dist.

*Optional; use thumb on 6th string throughout.

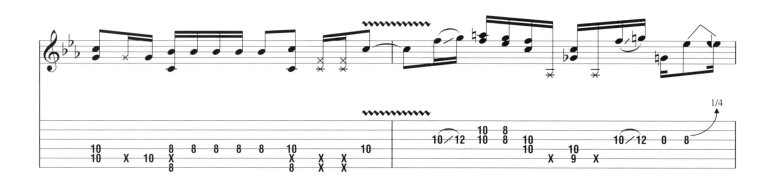

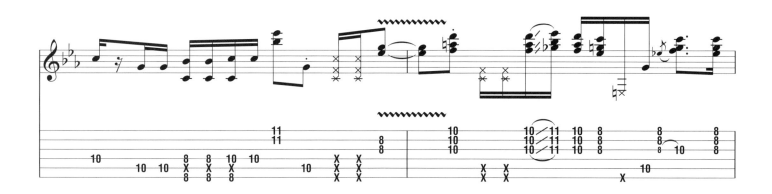

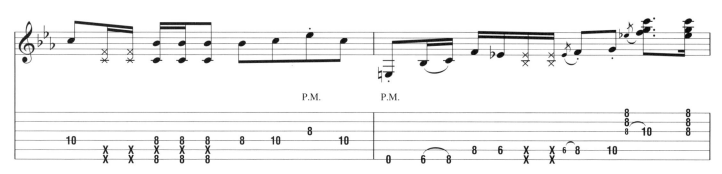

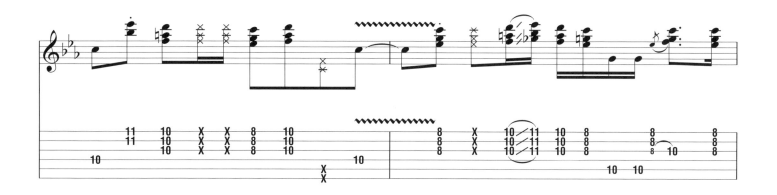

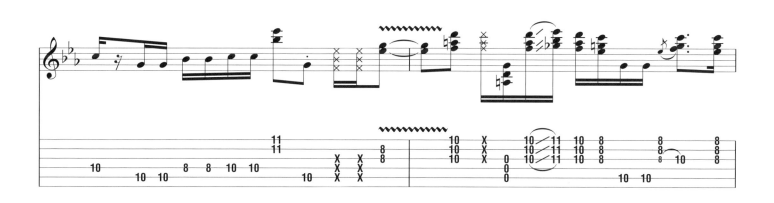

1. My   way

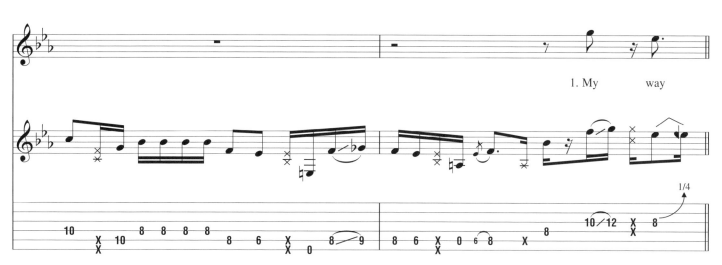

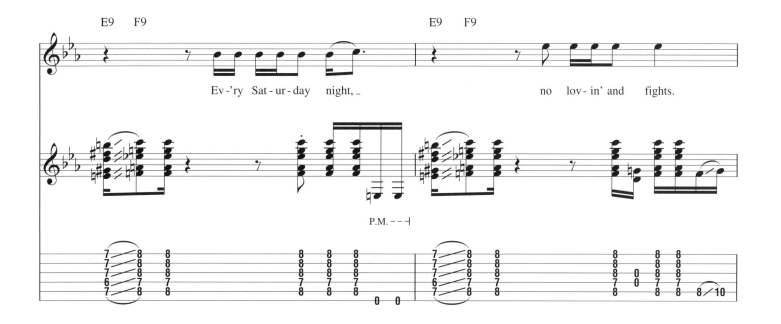

Ev-'ry Sat-ur-day night, _____ no lov-in' and fights.

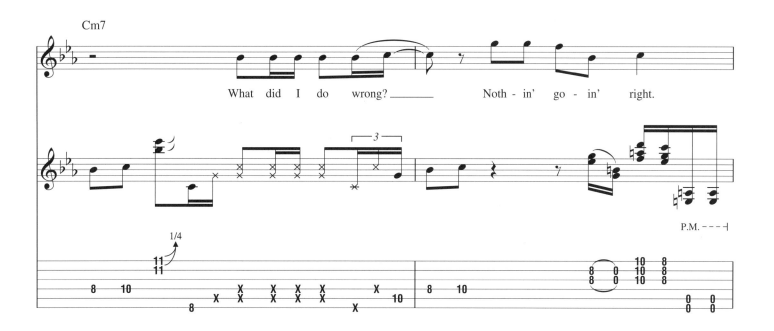

What did I do wrong? _____ Noth-in' go-in' right.

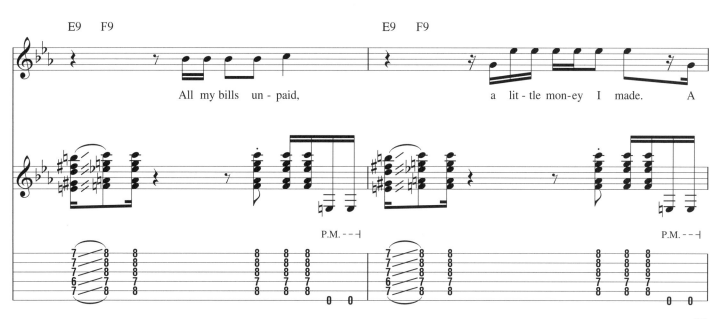

All my bills un-paid, a lit-tle mon-ey I made. A

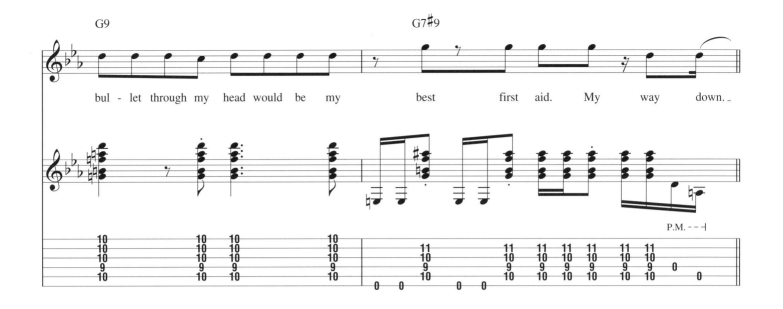

Chorus

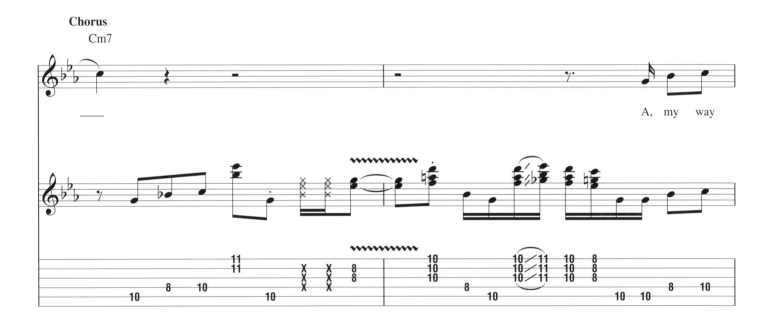

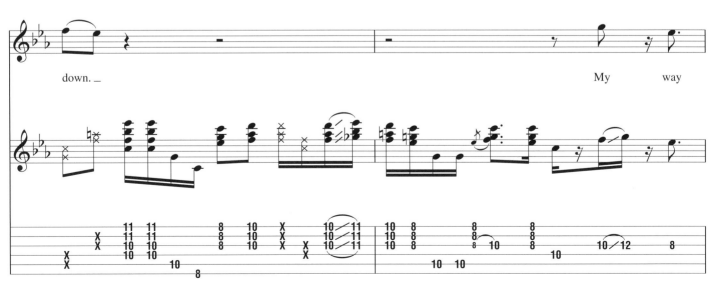

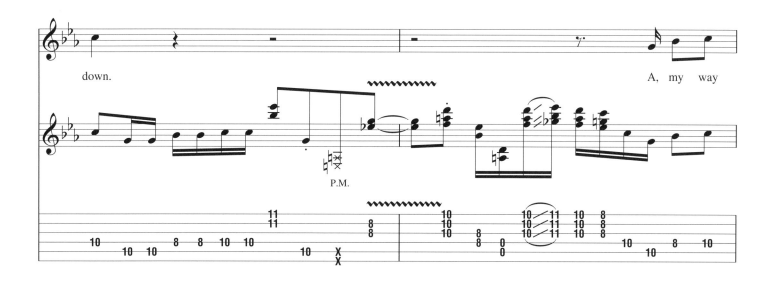

down.

A, my way

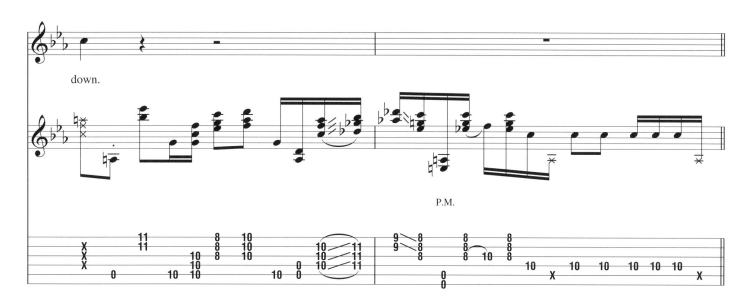

down.

P.M.

Guitar Solo

Cm7

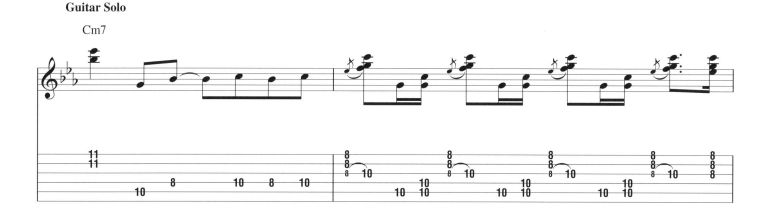

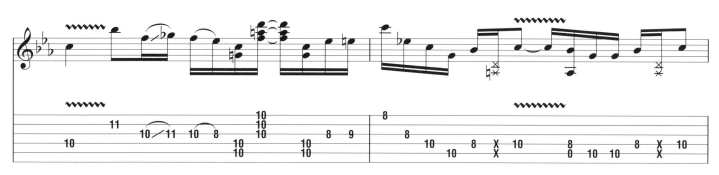

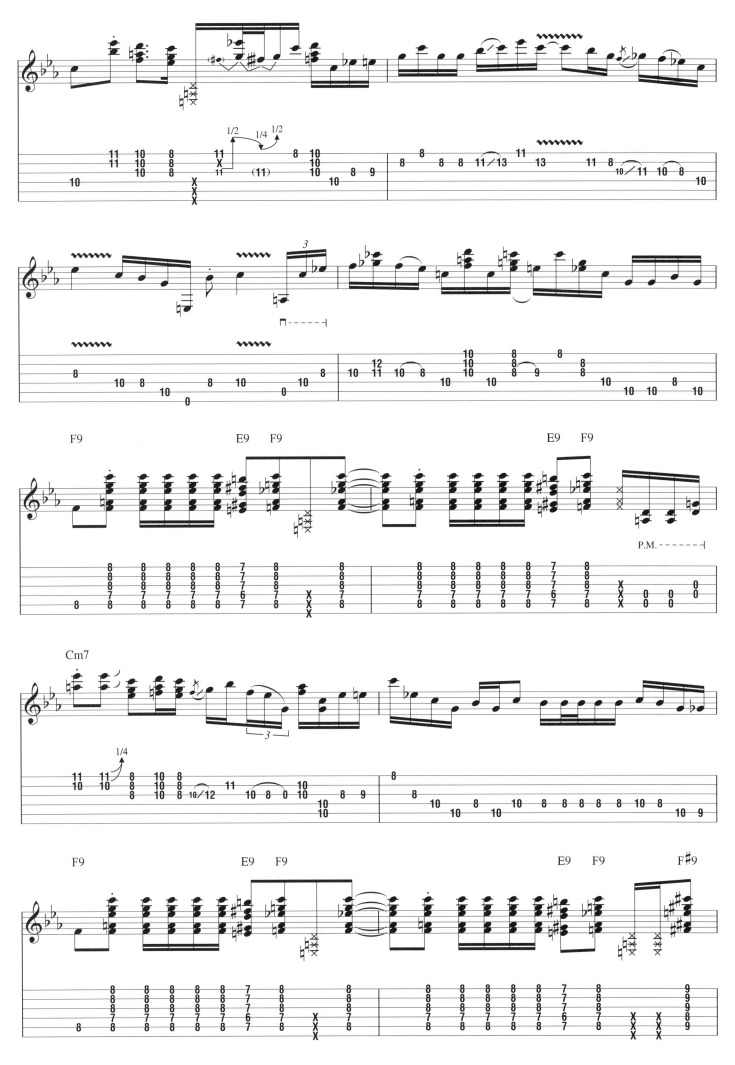

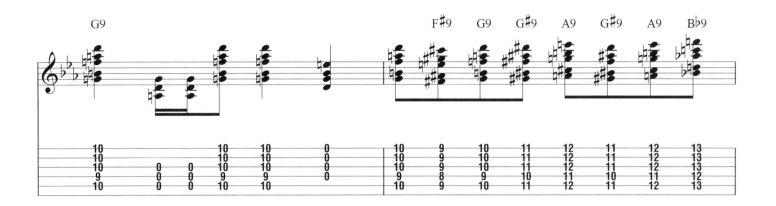

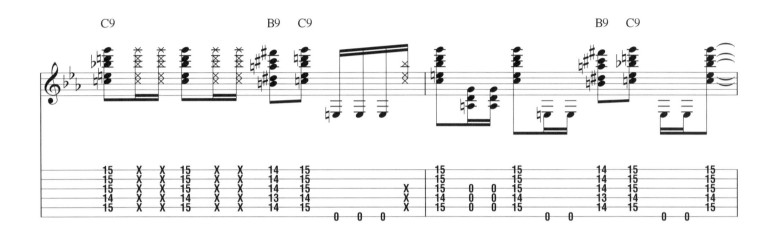

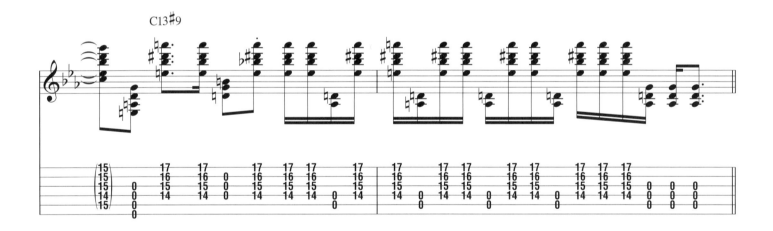

Guitar Solo

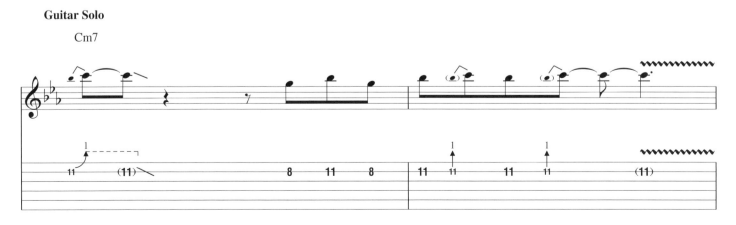

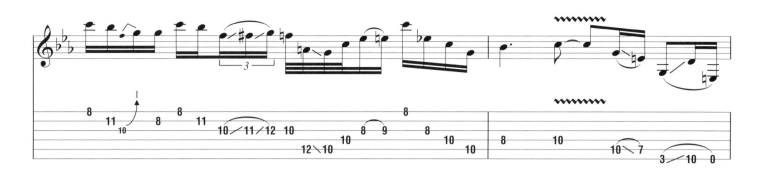

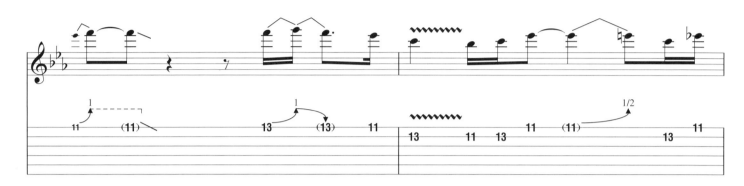

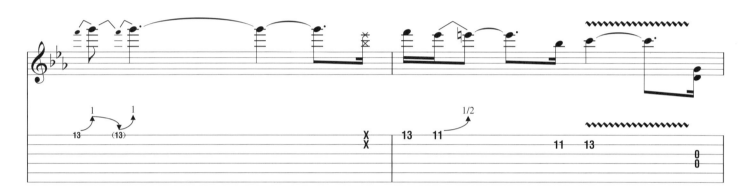

F9

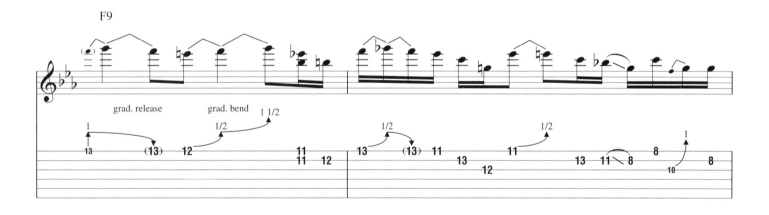

Cm7

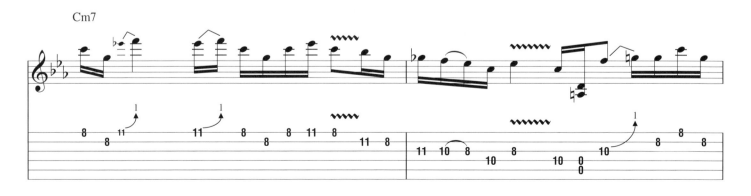

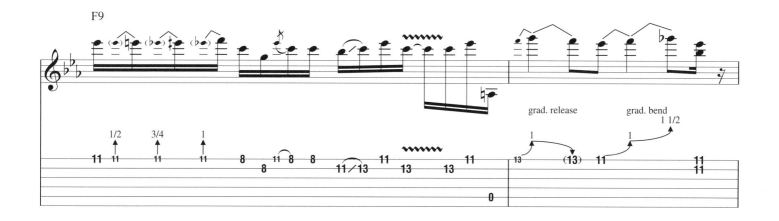

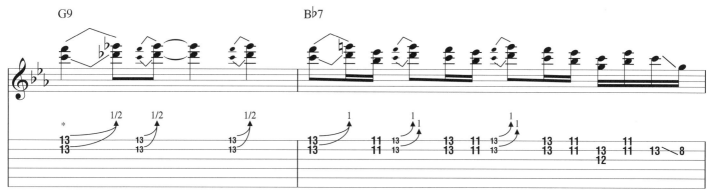

*Bend both notes w/ same finger, next 2 meas.

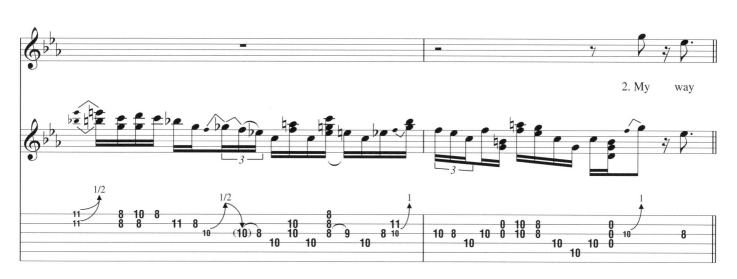

Outro

Cm7

My way down, ___

___ my way down. ___

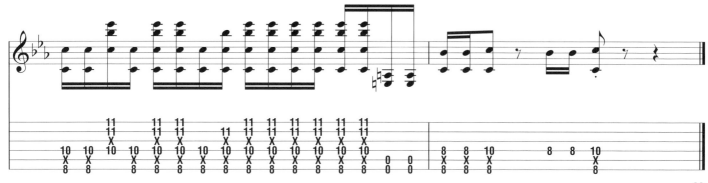

Never Make Your Move Too Soon

Words and Music by Will Jennings and Nesbert Hooper

Fm7

Land - lord said you moved a - way. _____

Left me all _____ those bills to pay. _____ Look out, _____

G7   C7

_____ ba - by.   Nev - er make your _____ move too

Fm7

soon. _____

52

Verse

3. I've been to Spain, To - ky - o, Af - ri - ca, O - hi - o. I nev - er tried to make the news. I'm just a man who plays the blues.

D.S. al Coda

Interlude
A tempo

Outro-Guitar Solo

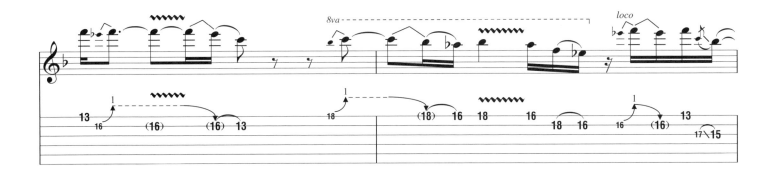

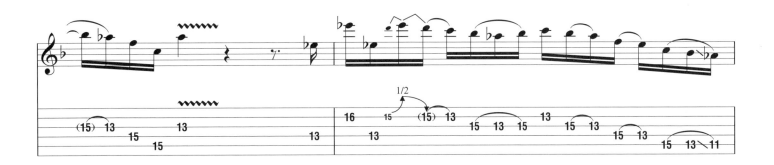

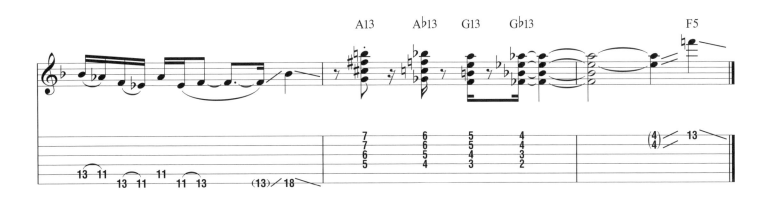

Additional Lyrics

2. Left me with all your credit cards.
    This life in Vegas sure ain't hard.
    Ran it up to fifty grand.
    Cash it in, in my hand.
    That kind of word can get around,
    Make a lost love come up a found.
    I hear you knockin' at my door,
    You're not livin' here no more.
    Look out, baby. Never make your move too soon.

3. I've been to Spain, Tokyo, Africa, Ohio.
    I never tried to make the news.
    I'm just a man who plays the blues.
    I take my lovin' ev'rywhere.
    I come back, they still don't care.
    One love ahead, one behind.
    One on my arm, one on my mind.
    Look out, baby. Oh, yeah.
    Oh, never make your move too soon.

Phone Booth

Words and Music by Robert Cray, Dennis Walker, Richard Cousins and Michael Vannice

Intro
Moderately ♩ = 120

$ Verse

1. I'm ___ in a (3.) phone booth, ba - by;
2., 4. *See additional lyrics*

num-bers ___ scratched

on the wall. ___   I'm ___ in a phone booth, ba - by;

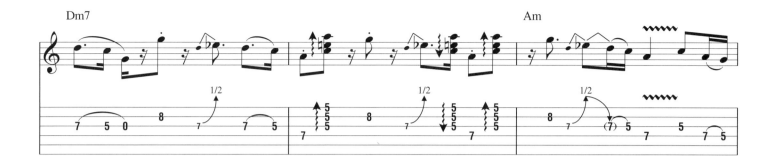

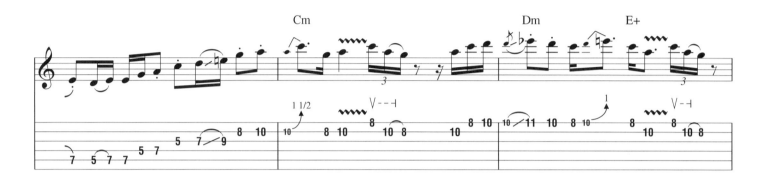

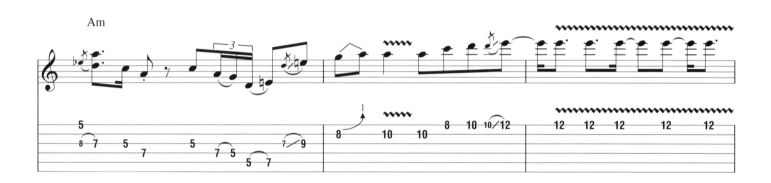

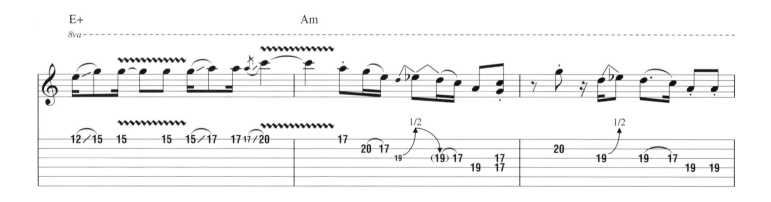

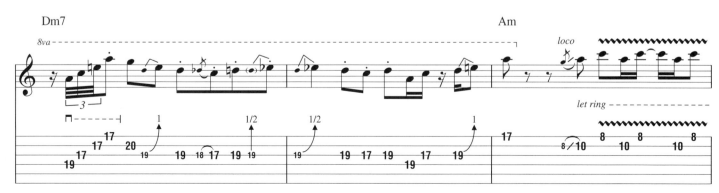

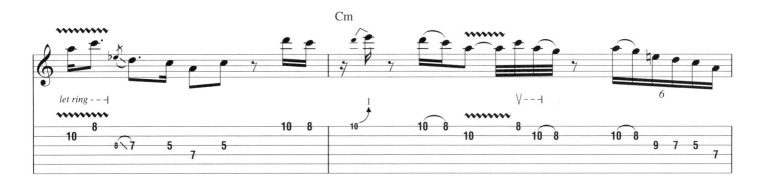

D.S. al Coda
(take repeat)

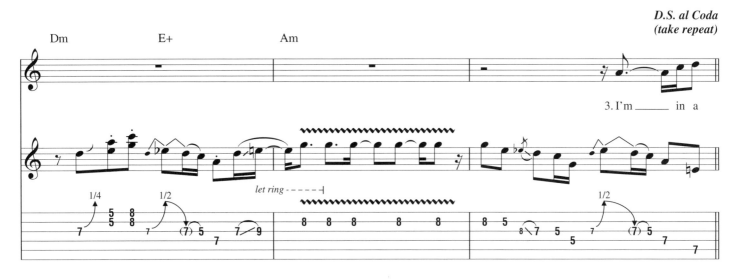

3. I'm ____ in a

⊕ **Coda**

Outro-Guitar Solo

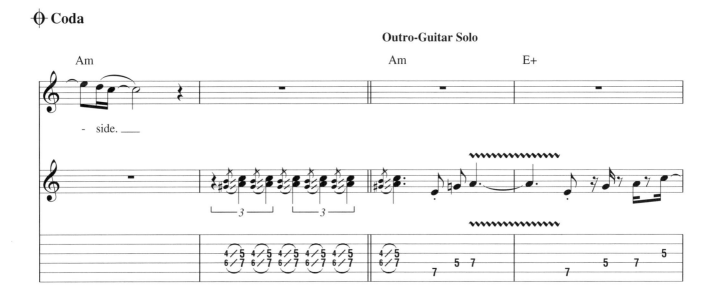

- side. ____

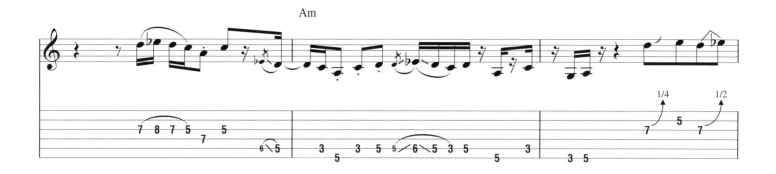

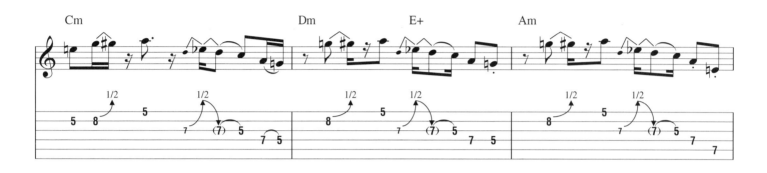

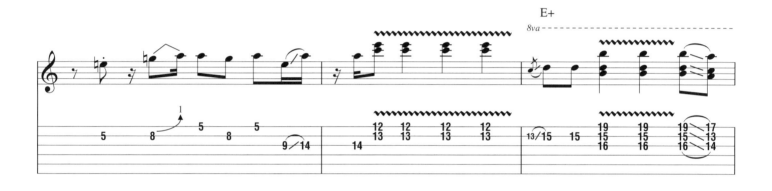

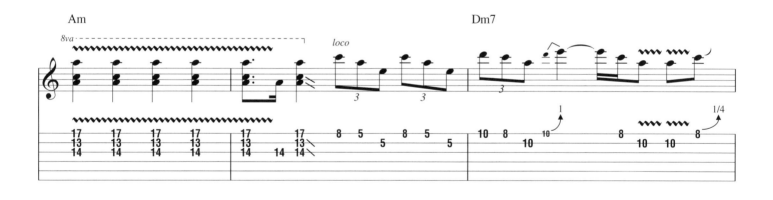

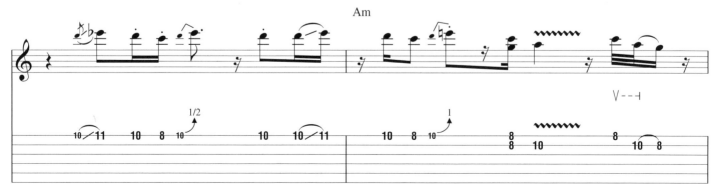

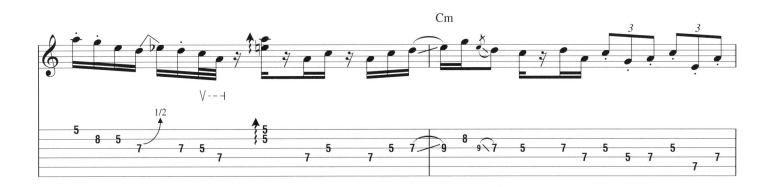

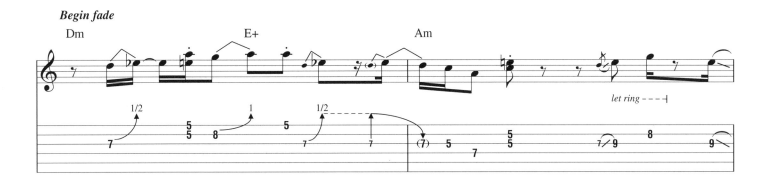

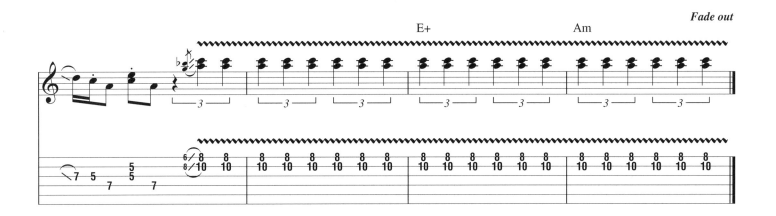

Additional Lyrics

2. Been walkin' all day; old friends I can't find.
   Hearts so cold, had to buy me some wine.
   Callin' you, baby, took my very last dime.

4. Said, "Call Big Rita anytime, day or night."
   You know I'm broke and I'm cold, baby,
   And I hope you'll treat me right.
   I'm in a phone booth, baby,
   With a cold wind right outside.

Rock Me Right

Words and Music by Tom Hambridge

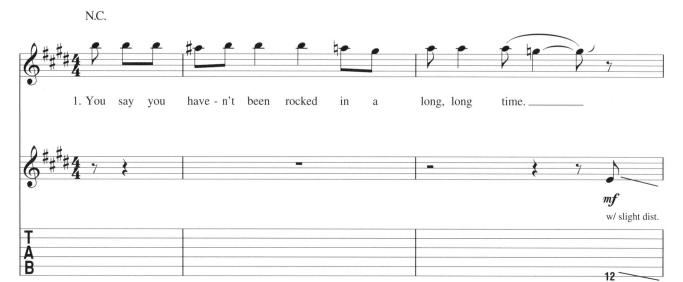

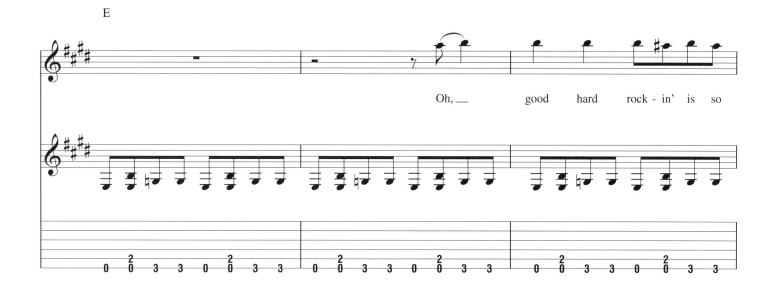

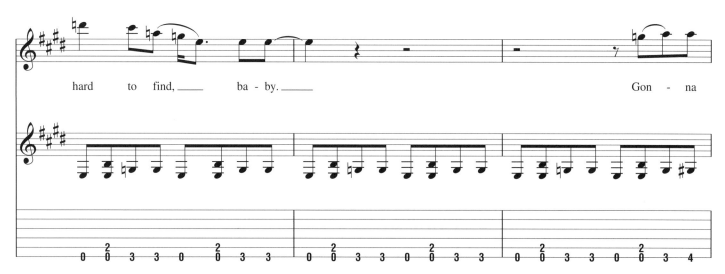

A

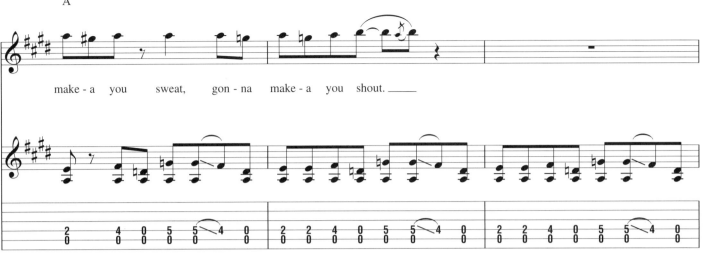

make - a you sweat, gon - na make - a you shout. _____

E

Oh, your home - made _ lov - in' done knocked me out, _____ ba - by. _

Verse

E

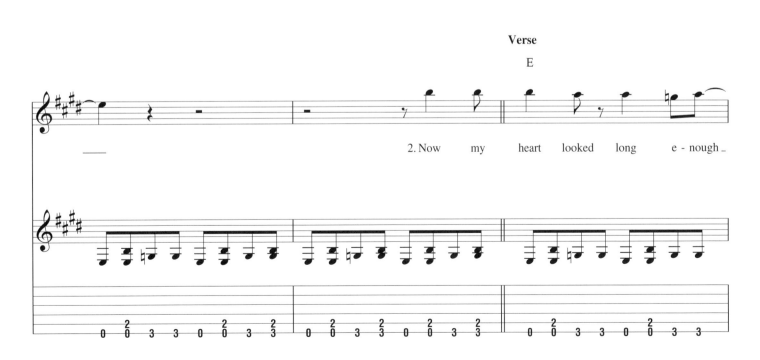

_____ 2. Now my heart looked long e - nough _

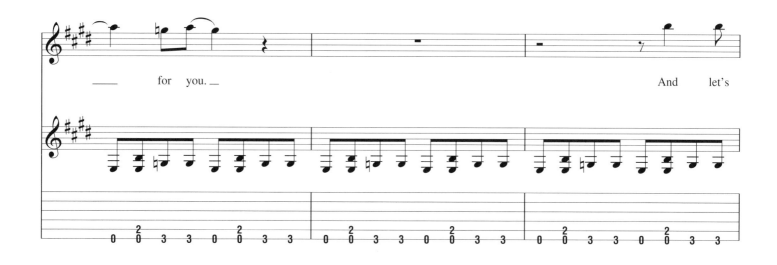

for you. ___ And let's

see if you know ___ what I'm fix - in' to do, ___ ba - by. ___

Now you wan - na lit - tle love, that's ___ al - right. ___

Oh, your fruit ain't-a rot-ten, it's oh,

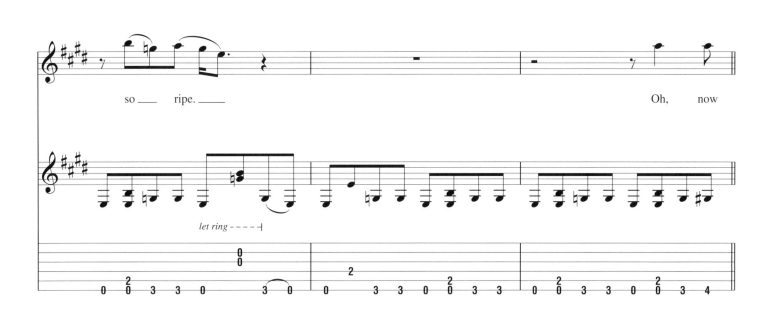

so ___ ripe. ___ Oh, now

Pre-Chorus

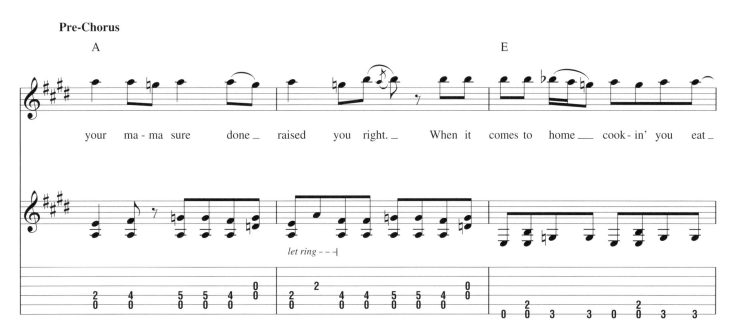

your ma-ma sure done ___ raised you right. ___ When it comes to home ___ cook-in' you eat ___

rock   me   right, ___   I'm   gon - na show you how to

rock   me   right.   Rock   me   right

Guitar Solo

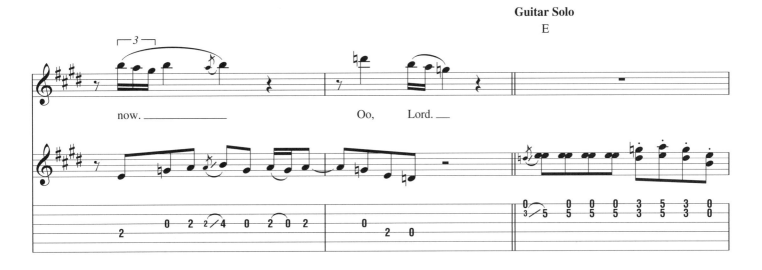

now. _____   Oo,   Lord. ___

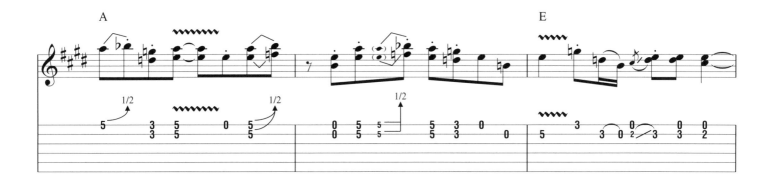

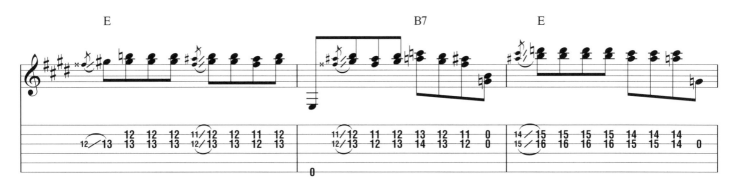

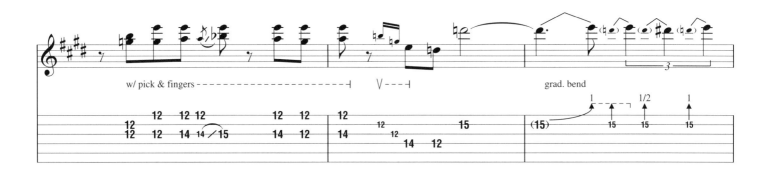

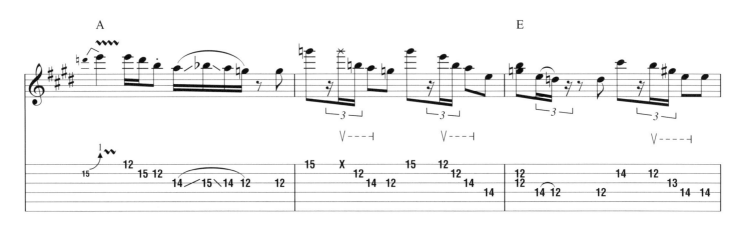

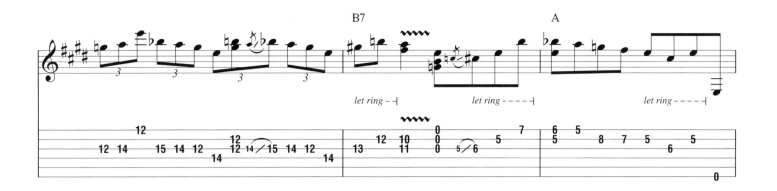

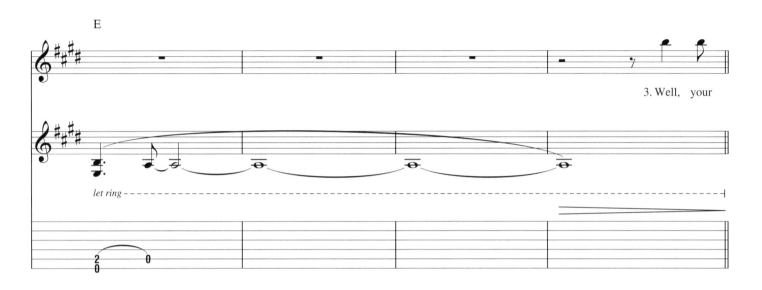

3. Well, your

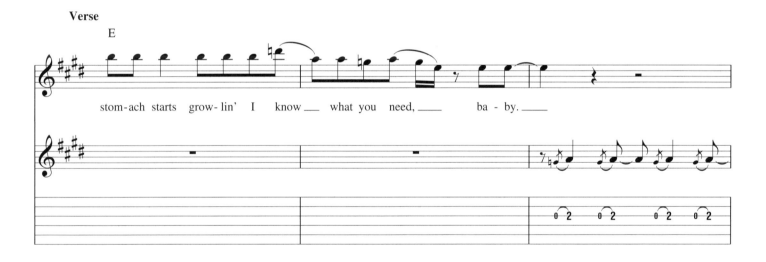

stom-ach starts grow-lin' I know ___ what you need, ___ ba - by. ___

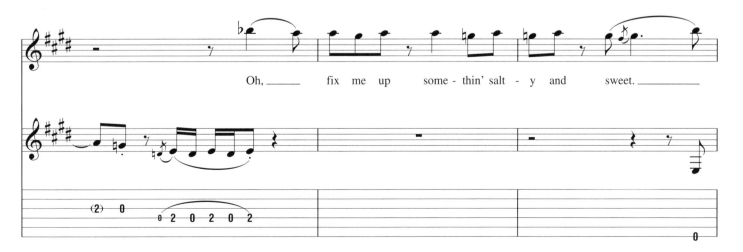

Oh, ___ fix me up some - thin' salt - y and sweet. ___

Oh, now home - made cook - in' al - ways

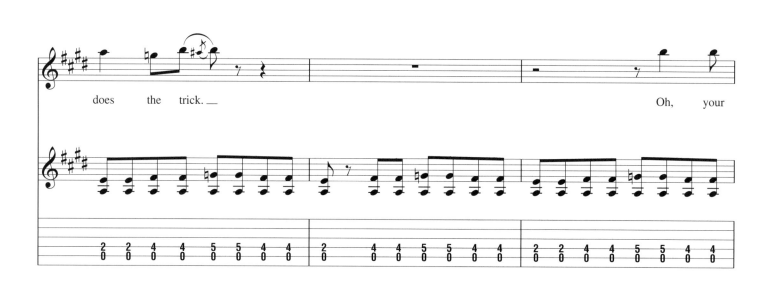

does the trick. ___ Oh, your

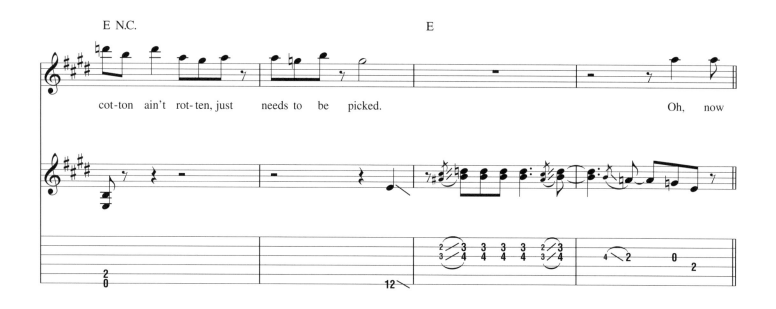

cot-ton ain't rot-ten, just needs to be picked. Oh, now

your ma - ma sure done — raised you right. — When it comes to home — cook - in' you eat

let ring - - -|

ev - 'ry bite. — Take your sweet time, got all night. _____

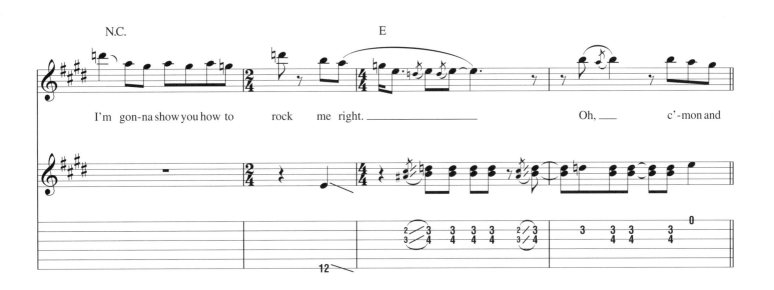

I'm gon-na show you how to rock me right. _____ Oh, ___ c'-mon and

Chorus

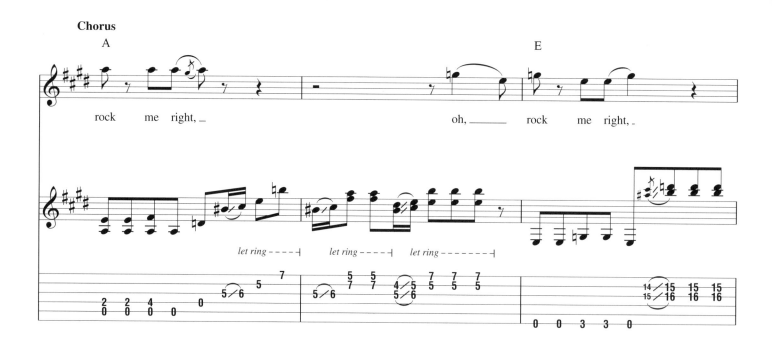

rock   me   right, ___   oh, _____ rock   me   right, _

rock   me   right. __

I'm   gon - na   show   you   how   to   rock   me   right.

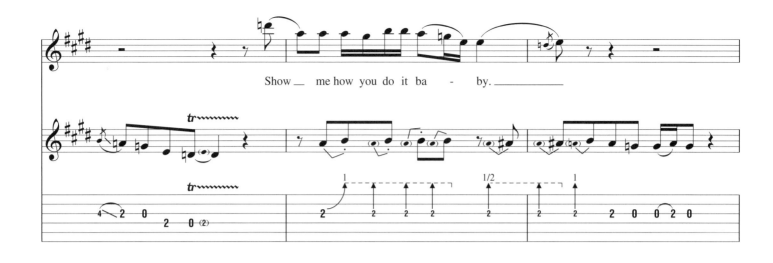

Show __ me how you do it ba - by. _____

Outro-Guitar Solo

E

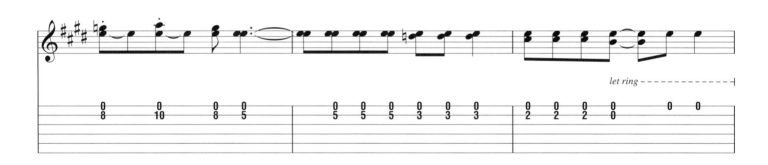

Oh. ____

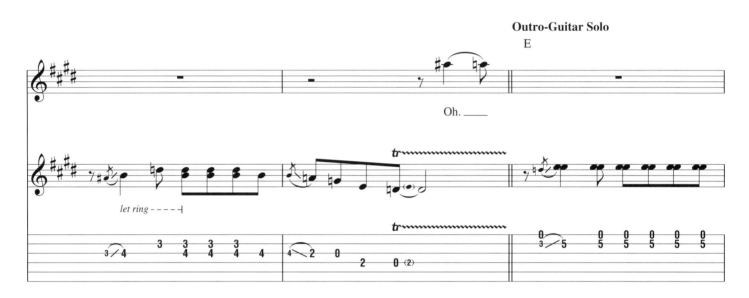

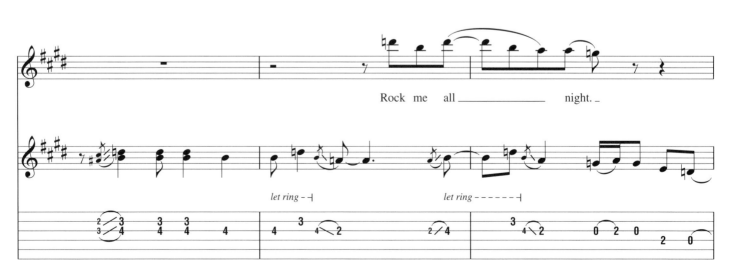

Rock me all _____ night. _

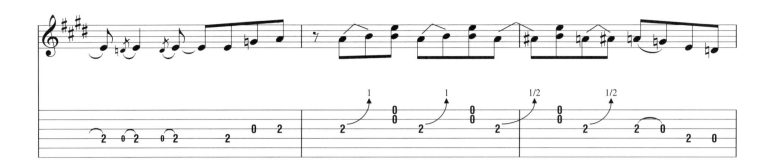

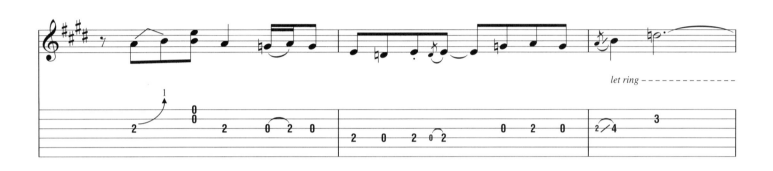

Begin fade

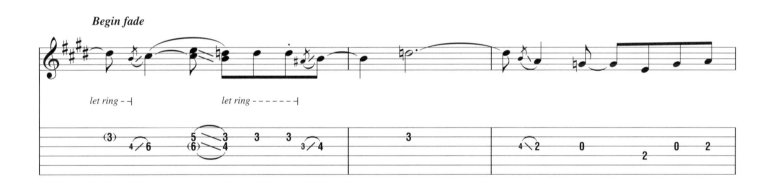

Fade out

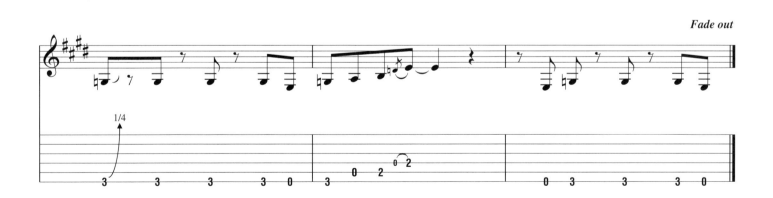

Mama Talk to Your Daughter

Words and Music by J.B. Lenoir and Alex Atkins

Verse

Ma - ma, pa - pa, please talk   to your daugh-ter for me. _____   Ma-

\- ma, pa - pa, please talk   to your daugh-ter for me. _____   She done made _

_____ me love her   and I ain't gon-na leave   her be. _____

w/ dist.

Interlude

Verse

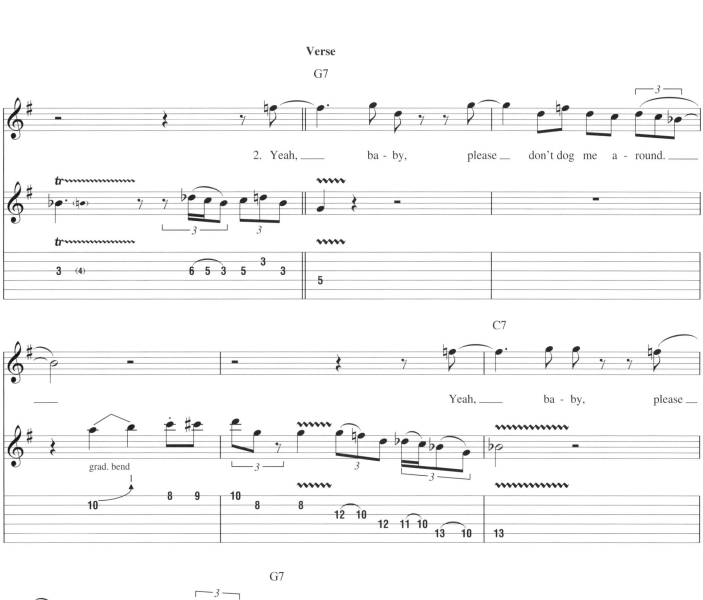

2. Yeah, ____ ba - by, please ____ don't dog me a - round. ____

Yeah, ____ ba - by, please ____

grad. bend

____ don't dog me a - round. ____

If you don't

quit your fool - in', put you six feet in the ground. ____

P.M.

Chorus

Guitar Solo

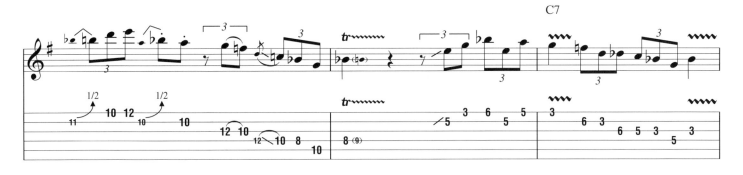

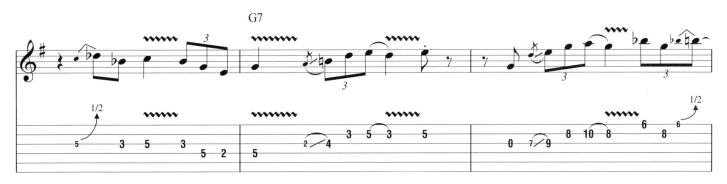

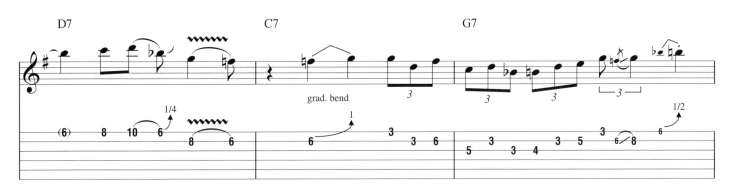

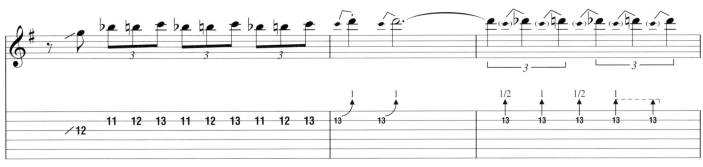

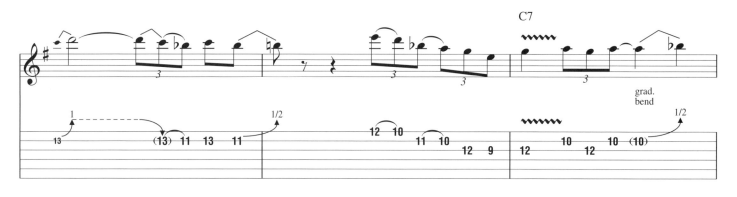

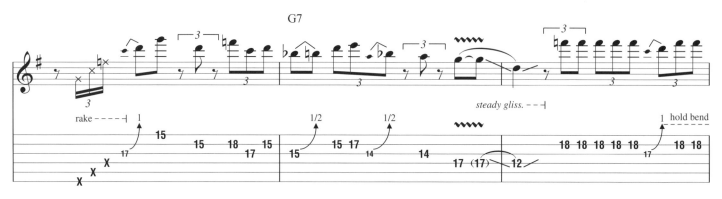

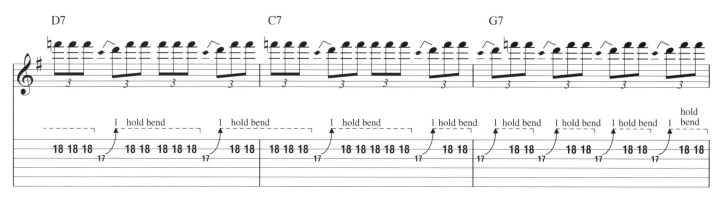

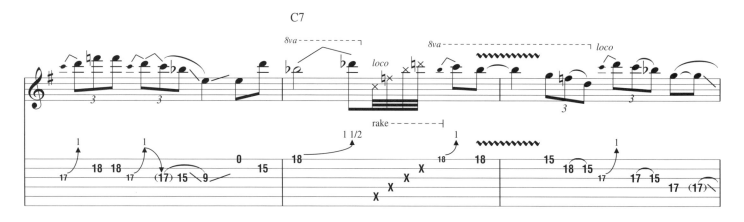

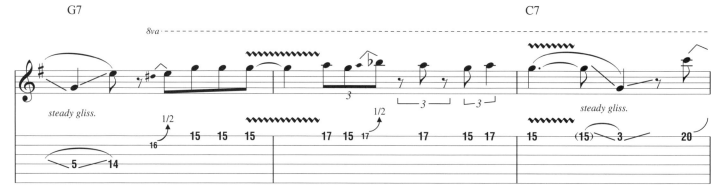

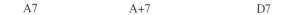

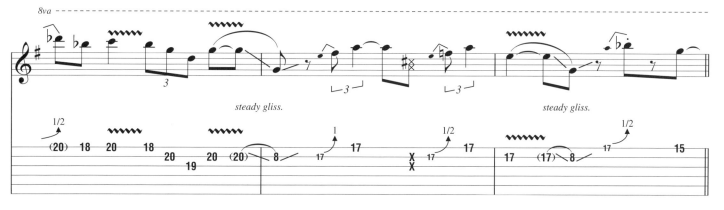

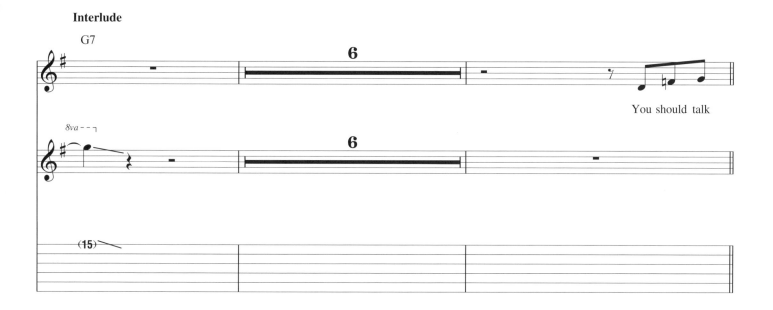

Interlude

You should talk

Chorus

to   your   daugh - ter.   You should talk   to   your   daugh - ter. ____

____ You should talk   to your daugh - ter. _____   You should talk   to your daugh - ter. ___

She done made ____ me love her and I ain't gon - na leave her be. ____

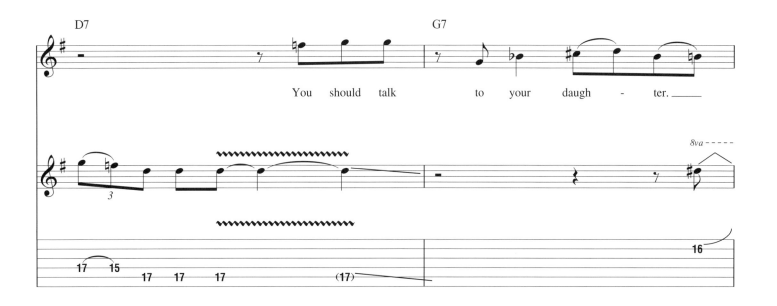

You should talk to your daugh - ter. ____

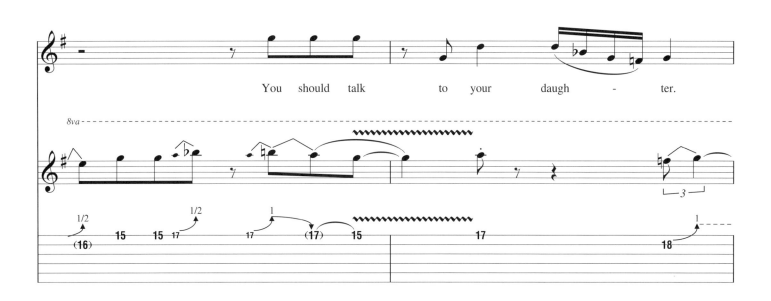

You should talk to your daugh - ter.

You should talk to your daugh - ter. You should talk

to your daugh - ter.   She done made ___ me love her and I

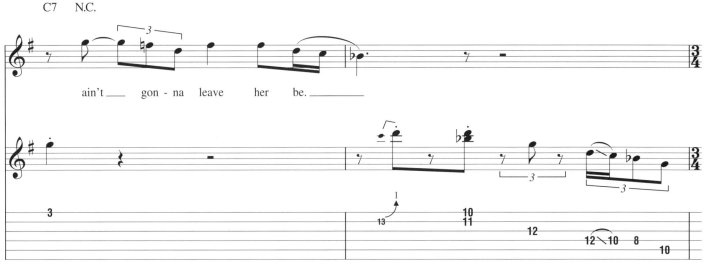

ain't ___ gon - na leave her be. ___

Free time ($\sqrt{3} = \sqrt{3}$)

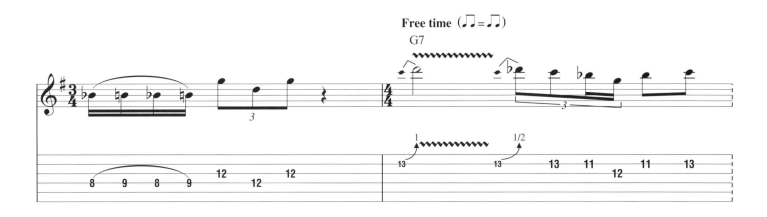

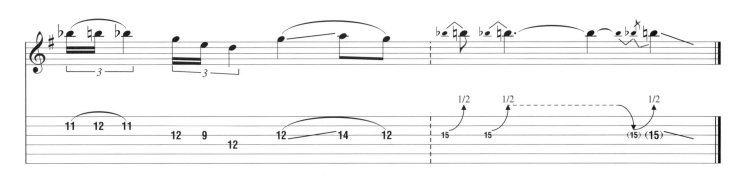